COURAGEOUS COMPANIONS

EXPLORING EFFECTIVE LEADERSHIP PRACTICES THROUGH POPULAR CULTURE

Series Editor: Michael Urick

The aim of this series is to examine modern and innovative business theories and methods via relatable popular cultural themes. The books will provide academically rigorous and credible applications and solutions to practitioners and upper level business students, in a format designed to be highly engaging and effective

Titles in Exploring Effective Leadership Practices Through Popular Culture

A Manager's Guide to Using the Force: Leadership Lessons From a Galaxy Far Far Away
Michael Urick

Leadership in Middle Earth: Theories and Applications for Organizations
Michael Urick

Leadership Insights for Wizards and Witches
Aditya Simha

Leaders Assemble! Leadership in the MCU
Gordon B. Schmidt and Sy Islam

Bend the Knee or Seize the Throne: Leadership Lessons From Westeros
Nathan Tong and Michael Urick

Forthcoming

Against All Odds: Leadership and the Handmaid's Tale
Cristina de Mello-e-Souza Wildermuth

COURAGEOUS COMPANIONS

Followership in Doctor Who

BY

KIMBERLY YOST
Pennsylvania Western University, USA

United Kingdom – North America – Japan
India – Malaysia – China

Emerald Publishing Limited
Emerald Publishing, Floor 5, Northspring, 21-23 Wellington Street, Leeds LS1 4DL

First edition 2024

Reprints and permissions service
Contact: www.copyright.com

British Library Cataloguing in Publication Data
A catalogue record for this book is available from the British Library

ISBN: 978-1-83753-987-1 (Print)
ISBN: 978-1-83753-984-0 (Online)
ISBN: 978-1-83753-986-4 (Epub)

INVESTOR IN PEOPLE

This book is dedicated to everyone who strives for the courage to laugh hard, run fast, and be kind.

CONTENTS

ABOUT THE AUTHOR

Kimberly Yost writes about the intersection of popular culture and leadership to discover how popular culture influences our understanding of leaders and the practice of leadership. She is the author of *From Starship Captains to Galactic Rebels: Leaders in Science Fiction Television*, co-editor of *Leadership, Popular Culture, and Social Change* with Kristin M.S. Bezio, and contributed to various edited volumes, including *Gender, Media, and Organization: Mis(s)Representations of Women Leaders and Managers, Leadership, Populism, and Resistance, The Embodiment of Leadership, The Routledge Companion to Leadership*, and *The Sage Encyclopedia of Leadership*. She is an editorial board member for the *Interdisciplinary Journal of Leadership Studies*. Dr Yost is an Assistant Professor at Pennsylvania Western University, California Campus, USA teaching management, organizational behavior, teamwork, and leadership courses.

You can connect with Dr Yost on LinkedIn or her website at www. kimberlyyost.com

PREFACE

As a scholar who uses popular culture narratives – and particularly science fiction narratives – to explore concepts about leadership and organizations, I have always wanted to write about the *Doctor Who* series. While I'm not the ultimate Whovian, I enjoy the show very much. But for many years I just couldn't seem to find my way into the connection between The Doctor and leadership.

In the Fall of 2022, as I was preparing my syllabus for a class on teamwork and leadership, I had a moment of clarity when developing a module on followership. I had been thinking about the chronicles of The Doctor from the wrong perspective. I discovered the series is properly examined from the perspective of the Companions. The lessons to be learned come from Rose Tyler, Martha Jones, Donna Noble, Amy Pond, Rory Williams, Clara Oswald, Bill Potts, Yasmin Khan, Ryan Sinclair, River Song, Wilfred Mott, Harriet Jones, Captain Jack Harkness, The Osgoods, and so many more. Without the wisdom and strength of the Companions, The Doctor would inflict even greater chaos and vengeance across the universe. There would be no one to rein in the excesses or offer alternative solutions and crucial assistance. There would be no one to balance the wrath with compassion. There would be no one who could courageously stand up to The Doctor. Followership was the key to understanding *Doctor Who*.

While learning about leadership through popular culture is relatively commonplace now, I knew there would be a challenge in finding anyone who may be interested in the connection between followership and popular culture beyond the idea of the hero's sidekick. Happily, a colleague recommended *A Manager's Guide to Using the Force: Leadership Lessons from a Galaxy Far Far Away* by Michael J. Urick and I discovered Emerald Publishing's series on Exploring Effective Leadership Practices Through Popular Culture. I knew this could be a great vehicle to share my ideas and enthusiasm for the series and connect it to followership theory.

I am fortunate Michael Urick and Fiona Allison at Emerald Publishing agreed with me, and I hope you do, too. Enjoy!

Kimberly Yost

Spring 2023

ACKNOWLEDGMENTS

I would like to thank family, friends, colleagues, students, and the team at Emerald Publishing for their support in helping to make this book happen. All of you made a significant contribution to keeping me motivated and focused on the project. Research and writing can be a lonely endeavor that isolates us from our normal relationships and routines. But when I did pop back up into the world, you were there. Your enthusiasm for the project gave me the courage to move forward. Thank you.

WHAT IS FOLLOWERSHIP AND WHY IS IT IMPORTANT?

Followership as a separate concept within leadership studies gained prominence in the 1990s and has evolved over the past few decades into an indispensable component of the discipline. Nevertheless, misunderstandings about followers and their relationship to leaders continue to flourish. Often when people think about followership, they consider the role of a follower as one of subservience or compliance and less significant or worthy than the role of a leader. There can be many other misconceptions, such as followers should strive to become leaders, followers are too cowardly to be leaders, and followers lack authority, dignity, or value (Hamlin, 2016). This is particularly true in the United States which has a cultural expectation of leaders being heroic individuals and followers passively carrying out orders or waiting for deliverance. But what we are learning is that followers are crucial for the success of leaders and their organizations. I endeavor to help you understand the critical role followers play in the process of leadership by examining followership through the popular BBC television series *Doctor Who* (1963–present).

But why *Doctor Who*?

Well, because it's much more fun to explore wonky academic theories and concepts through a television show, but it's also an opportunity to open our minds to the ways in which popular culture can influence how we think about followers and leaders. Works of fiction can have a wide audience and, in that way, become more influential than traditional academic research (Lewis et al., 2008). Moreover, popular culture narratives "shape and constitute our understanding of social and organizational life … [and are] a powerful tool for illustrating topics and concepts and for demonstrating the application of theory" (Huczynski & Buchanan, 2004, p. 708). In using an internationally known and beloved television series that has been produced for 60 years, we have an opportunity to explore these concepts and apply the theories by means of the shared experience of watching the show regardless of the time or place we occupy.

There is an added value of using visual narratives to explore followers and leaders because of the human element. The relationship between followers and leaders can be messy. There can be misunderstandings, hurt feelings, frustrations, annoyance, anger, and fear. These emotional conditions are more aptly depicted through visual stories. Students may be familiar with analyzing a written case study about a real-world situation so they can apply it to the concepts or theories within a course. Rarely is there any mention of the dreadfully difficult interpersonal challenges the protagonists experienced in resolving their conflict or overcoming their obstacles. If these difficulties are included, unpleasant or awkward moments may be toned-down as the successful resolution of the organizational problem is known and interpersonal conflicts can be largely dismissed in favor of celebrating the accomplishments of those involved. People are hardly ever acrimonious toward each other in written case studies. As we know, history is written by the privileged victors and those who dissent or are bad-tempered are seldom given a part in the narrative.

In a long-form visual narrative, such as a television series, we get to witness unpleasant or awkward moments. We see how the followers and leader navigate the highs and lows of their relationship as they seek to resolve problems. The ways in which followers challenge their leaders are given voice. We become aware of how their relationship grows and changes, as well as the doubts and fear every follower and leader experiences. Our empathetic capacities and moral imagination are activated through the immediacy of viewing the visual narrative. Importantly, in these narratives there can be failure to achieve a goal, which increases our understanding of how followers and leaders cope with loss, disappointment, and defeat.

There is also an advantage to using narratives specifically in the science fiction genre for an exploration of followers and leaders. As Sontag (1976) correctly noted, science fiction stories aren't about science – they're about disasters. Aliens invade. Planets are whisked away to another part of the universe. There are rifts in the time–space continuum threatening all existence. Through these disasters, science fiction stories clearly demonstrate crisis management and adaptive leadership behaviors. While The Doctor may use science and technology to solve a problem, they use those tools because there's a crisis and impending disaster.

Additionally, Roberts (2007) explains, science fiction allows us to contemplate our own world more fully through the stories of the fantastic. Protagonists in science fiction stories role model positive social behaviors that may be lacking in the real world. In *Doctor Who*, we encounter differences among companions and other-worldly species and can be motivated to accept and celebrate differences in our own circumstances. We are shown injustices across space and time and relate the experiences of the persecuted and exploited to the injustice we see in our contemporary world and can be inspired to act against those injustices. We witness problem-solving in creative and innovative ways that can lead us to consider our own abilities to meet challenges with determination and imagination and seek novel solutions to the issues that face our organizations and societies.

Most importantly, science fiction narratives reconcile the tensions between our rational and spiritual selves. They are a projection of our fears and our desires for the future. Do we envision a dystopian society based on oppression and authoritarianism as seen in *The Handmaid's Tale*, or a cooperative, inclusive democratic society such as the Federation in *Star Trek*?

The competing values of rational decision-making through logic and hard data against spiritual self-actualization and duty of care for others drives the greatest challenges that confront leaders and followers. This can be exemplified with the dilemma facing organizational leaders when they look at their poor financial data and are pressured into cutting their workforce which competes with their organizational culture of valuing their employees and caring about their well-being. Or perhaps an organization is dedicated to sustainability and green technology, but their data show they are failing in their efforts, or the processes are too costly to maintain in the long term. The Ninth Doctor puts a weary angry voice to this dilemma when he says, "This is my life. It's not fun. It's not smart. It's just me standing up making decisions because nobody else will" (*World War Three*, 2005).

What choices can we make now to bring about the future we desire? How can we find the balance between rationality and spirituality and integrate both into our daily lives and decision-making? Indeed, I maintain the competing values of adhering to logic and rationality versus adhering to what is morally right and serves others is the primary dilemma The Doctor faces in the series and the area where the Companions are most effective as courageous followers.

DESCRIBING FOLLOWERSHIP

To adequately describe followership, we need to also describe leadership. As with misconceptions about followership, there are also misconceptions about leadership. Northouse (2019) defines leadership as "a process whereby an individual influences a group of individuals toward a common goal" (p. 5). Yukl (2006) defines leadership as "the process of influencing others to understand and agree about what needs to be done and how to do it, and the process of facilitating individual and collective efforts to accomplish shared objectives" (p. 8). Most leadership theorists repeat the same key understanding that leadership is a process of exerting influence to reach a shared goal.

Keep in mind a process of influence takes effort over time and shouldn't be confused with the idea of just telling people what to do, nor involve a goal that only serves the leader's interests. It's also distinct from management in that leaders are tasked with developing a vision of the future – a projection of fears and desires that requires action and change – and gaining support for that change, while managers must deal with the day-to-day complexity of making the vision a reality (Kotter, 2001). Neither of the above definitions state a leader must be the boss, or male, or wealthy, or an extrovert, or any other misguided notion we may have about what constitutes a leader. The main consideration is for a leader to be able to hold some type of power that allows them to influence others toward achieving a goal.

The power to influence others can take several forms. What can be called "formal" or "legitimate" power stems from a leader having a title and the official authority to make decisions that affect others and their organizations or societies, such as a CEO, Archbishop, Prime Minister, Divisional Manager, or US Senator. Other power can be identified as "expert" or "referent". An expert can influence others due to their knowledge or experience, such as a climatologist speaking about the dangers of global climate change or a professional footballer explaining defensive strategies. Someone who holds referent power has influence because people admire them or hold them in esteem and are willing to listen to their wisdom and opinions, such as a tribal elder or a social media personality. In organizations, leaders often emerge through expert or referent power though they may hold a lower status position in the hierarchy, such as a technical specialist or administrative assistant.

Even those who do not hold a formal position of power in an organization or social system can develop visions for changes and gain support for those changes through the exercise of expert or referent power. This is the history of social justice initiatives from women's suffrage to civil rights to climate justice. From British suffragette Mrs Emmeline Pankhurst to US civil rights leader Reverend Dr Martin Luther King Jr to Swedish climate activist Greta Thunberg, we have seen how those with expert or referent power are able to influence others by sharing their vision which advocates for social justice and speaks to the desires we have for the future and not the fears.

What has often been missing in the definition of leadership as a process is the role that followership plays. Uhl-Bien et al. (2014) identify "leadership as a process that is co-created in social and relational interactions between people" (p. 83). In other words, leaders should not take on the function of leadership and insist they are solely responsible for identifying goals and implementing the process of influencing others, but understand their position is granted to them and the process of influence is shaped in tandem with their followers. There is a deference of authority and power given to leaders by followers, which can be taken back, whether they are in a formal position of power or are exercising expert or referent power. CEOs can be fired for not meeting the needs of shareholders. Politicians can be voted out for immoral or unethical behaviors. Social media influencers can lose their followers and their power in an instant by posting a socially or politically unacceptable tweet or TikTok video.

Leaders do require their followers to help them shape the leadership process. As Hamlin (2016) points out, followers are not the opposite of a leader, but complement the leader. Leaders must acknowledge their interdependent relationship with their followers and create opportunities for their followers in developing and implementing the leadership process of influence by employing the skills, qualities, and sensibilities followers possess. For leaders to be successful beyond the strictures of the hierarchy and compliant subordinates, followers must be willing to behave in ways that combine with the behaviors of leaders to create the leadership process and reach the desired objectives (Uhl-Bien et al., 2014).

This understanding gives us a foundation to identify that just as effective and successful leaders cannot singularly be defined by the place they inhabit in a hierarchy, neither can followers. Both roles are shaped by individual behaviors and the ways in which they interact in the process of achieving their objectives. Effective followers may be subordinates on an organizational chart but behave in supportive and self-directed ways that blend with the leader's behaviors to reach shared goals more efficiently and successfully.

But not all followers behave in equal or similar manners. Just as contingency theory suggests leaders alter their leadership style to fit a specific circumstance or the needs of an individual follower (Fiedler, 1964), followers can change their behaviors according to their interest in reaching a goal or the stage of their relationship with their leader. The dyadic relationship between leaders and followers is essential for shaping the leadership process and can be regarded as phases of development.

In the mid-1970s, the leader–member exchange (LMX) theory described the way in which leaders can build their relationships with followers through using their influence, with and without authority, and categorized those relationships as being an in-group, where the interpersonal relationship is strong and followers are engaged, and the out-group, where the interpersonal relationship is weaker and followers give minimal effort (Dansereau et al., 1975). This theory has been further developed over the decades and is connected to levels of communication between leaders and followers, job satisfaction, follower empowerment, and positive organizational behaviors (Northouse, 2019).

In the 1990s, LMX research focused on how the theory can be used for leadership making, where a leader endeavors to build strong in-group relationships with all followers and attempts to break the stigma of being in an out-group, which helps to engage all followers and increase the successful achievement of organizational goals. As advanced by Graen and Uhl-Bien (1995), leadership making has three phases where the relationship between leaders and followers moves from Stranger to Acquaintance to Partner. In the Stranger Phase, the relationship is low quality where the focus is on self-interest and depends on following formal roles and abiding by organizational rules. It is similar to the previous concept of being in an out-group, but there is an implicit understanding that followers are not stuck in the out-group and are able to move away from this phase. In the Acquaintance Phase, the relationship between leader and follower improves as they begin to know each other a little more through testing a leader's willingness to develop the follower and a follower's interest in new challenges. If successful, the focus for each is a mix of self-interest but moving toward the needs of the organization. In the Partner Phase, the relationship has matured, and they experience high-quality exchanges. This phase is characterized by mutual trust, respect, and reciprocal influence. Leaders and followers feel an obligation to each other, though their primary focus is on the interests of the organization (Graen & Uhl-Bien, 1995). As seen through the three phases of relationship building in LMX theory, we begin to understand how interpersonal relationships grounded in the benefit of mutual influence and the knowledge that followers complement leaders connects to the ability of leaders and followers to co-construct the leadership process.

TYPES OF FOLLOWERS

In addition to describing the function of followers and their relationship to leaders, it's also important to describe the different types of followers. Just as leaders can reflect upon their strengths to shape their leadership style, followers engage in the same kinds of reflections to determine how they view themselves as followers and their followership style. "Different followers affect leaders in different ways" (Matshoba-Ramuedzisi et al., 2022, para. 9), and several theorists have developed typologies for the kinds of followers present in an organization. Notably, there is a common thread among the theories advocating for active, engaged, independent followers to give leaders and organizations the greatest advantage.

In 1965, Abraham Zaleznik described followers in terms of dominance/submission and active/passive. His thesis discussed followers as those who want to control their boss or be controlled by them, and those who want to participate or do nothing. He grouped followers into categories of impulsive, compulsive, masochistic, and withdrawn (Zaleznik, 1965). Clearly, his thinking is influenced by the psychologist Sigmund Freud, but his base argument of encouraging leaders to know deeply about their followers from a psychoanalytical viewpoint was a practical early theory for increasing an organization's competitive advantage.

In the early 1990s, Robert Kelley was at the vanguard of followership theory in the face of prevailing leader-centric thought for developing organizational capacities for competitive advantages. He identified five different types of followers based on their level of engagement and their inclination for independent critical thought. Kelley's description of follower styles was alienated, sheep, yes-people, survivors, and exemplary followers. His basic argument was to encourage people to not follow blindly, but to use their critical thinking skills and examine their self-motivation skills to determine the behaviors and level of engagement they should demonstrate as followers (Kelley, 1992).

Barbara Kellerman (2007) uses the single attribute of a follower's level of engagement in developing her typology. Her categories include isolates, bystanders, participants, activists, and die hards. Kellerman (2007) recognizes that within our contemporary knowledge worker economy, followers view themselves "as free agents, not as dependent underlings" (p. 86). Followers are willing to support good leaders and withhold their support from bad leaders, furthering the understanding of leadership as a co-constructed process of influence. Leaders can quickly determine the potential for fostering a strong interpersonal relationship to advance organizational goals by identifying the level of engagement a follower exhibits (Kellerman, 2007).

The followership typology we are primarily concerned with in this book is that of Ira Chaleff (2009) and his considerations of courageous followers. Chaleff groups followers into four quadrants based on their support for the leader and how likely they are to challenge the leader. These quadrants are Resource, Individualist, Implementer, and Partner.

The fourth quadrant is for the Resource, who demonstrates low support and low challenge. These followers can be likened to isolates or alienated types, but they don't necessarily display overt negativity. They are present but do no more than the minimum expectations and try to avoid attention. There could be external reasons for their behavior, such as someone with increased family obligations or interests outside of work like community volunteerism or pursuing higher education. It's possible for this type of follower to re-engage and move to another quadrant when their other obligations or interests decrease (Chaleff, 2009).

The next type of follower per Chaleff (2009) is the Individualist. This follower gives low support to the leader and frequently challenges them. They can be described as confrontational and self-assured in their beliefs. While these people may balance the tendency of a group to fall into groupthink, where too much harmony or like-minded thinking can impair the decision-making process, they can be annoying and are often marginalized by the leader and fellow group members.

The second quadrant represents the Implementer who shows high support for the leader, but they are not likely to challenge or criticize. They are dependable and don't need a lot of oversight to get the job done. They may be a team player and advocate for the leader and their policies, but they are respectful of authority and simply reinforce the leader without question. While this type of follower may seem ideal, their lack of willingness to engage in healthy dialogue when they disagree or see problems with a leader's direction prevents a fully effective interpersonal relationship and leadership process (Chaleff, 2009).

The final quadrant is for the Partner. This is a follower who is highly supportive but isn't shy about challenging a leader's behaviors or policies. Obviously, this is closely aligned to the concept of a mature partner in LMX theory and implies a strong interpersonal relationship based on mutual respect, trust, and interdependence. Partners are committed to the purpose and mission and willing to take risks. They are able to confront sensitive issues and hold themselves and others accountable. In most ways, this is the ideal courageous follower as the Partner's behaviors complement the leader's behaviors (Chaleff, 2009).

In addition to his model of the types of followers and their relationship to their leader, Chaleff (2009) argues for a set of behaviors followers can develop to benefit their leaders, organizations, societies, and themselves. The concept is founded on courage and explores how followers can hold themselves and leaders accountable to impede and prevent the abuse of power. The five dimensions of courageous followership include The Courage to Assume Responsibility, The Courage to Serve, The Courage to Challenge, The Courage to Participate in Transformation, and The Courage to Take Moral Action. These dimensions are supported by two enriching behaviors on the part of leaders, The Courage to Speak to the Hierarchy and The Courage to Listen to Followers. As Chaleff (2009) writes, "by weaving the principle of accountable followership into our culture at every level, the fabric will become strong enough to resist the periodic attempts of individual leaders to emboss it with their own martial coat of arms" (pp. xxvii–xix). In other words, through embedding accountability into the culture of an organization or society, courageous followers can constrain autocrats and tyrants.

Exploring what it takes to be a follower is increasingly important. Our current organizational, social, and political landscapes are rife with leaders who are impulsive and arrogant. Narcissism has seemingly become an acceptable leadership characteristic in the 21st century. Yet, the outcomes have been clear throughout history – this type of leader fails when their followers refuse to stand up to them with the courage it takes to rein in the excesses and unethical behaviors. Conversely, good leaders also fail when their followers lack the courage to stand up *for* them and support the goals that will increase the organization's effectiveness or competitive advantage. "The most capable followers in the world will fail if they gripe about their leaders but don't help them improve" (Chaleff, 2009, p. xix). It's easy to criticize when a leader fails to bring forth their vision as quickly or effortlessly as we would like. It's necessary for courageous followers to not be dissuaded and continue to stand up for their leader and help them improve their ability to bring about change.

But how might we find the way to become a better follower without falling into the traps of sycophancy or contentiousness? How might we look at the relationship of leaders and followers in a way that can set aside our real-world assumptions and biases? We find the opportunity in exploring popular culture stories and fictional characters who take the developmental journey of followership and the fictional leaders who are changed by their relationships with their followers. We learn these lessons with them and can be motivated by the modeling of their positive behaviors.

A BRIEF INTRODUCTION TO *DOCTOR WHO*

Doctor Who is a BBC television program that first aired from 1963 to 1989 and returned in 2005 to the present. The story centers on The Doctor, a Time Lord from the planet Gallifrey. Time Lords are an ancient race who are self-appointed protectors of time across the universe and control the technology for time travel. At the outset of the narrative, The Doctor hurriedly leaves Gallifrey in the middle of a war with their archenemies, the Daleks, in a TARDIS (Time and Relative Dimension in Space), a machine that allows The Doctor to travel in time and space. When The Doctor visits Earth, the TARDIS malfunctions and now appears only as a blue police box typically seen in the United Kingdom in the early 1960s. The Doctor travels with various people, collectively known as Companions, in their adventures across the universe. They battle aliens, solve mysteries, save planets, liberate the oppressed, protect the powerless, correct historical anomalies, and, above all, defend Earth.

The Doctor's age is a contentious subject but suffice to say it's at least a few millennia. The Doctor reaches this great age by being a Time Lord who can regenerate physically and inhabits various bodies – old/young, male/female, white/black – over the course of the series. Each incarnation of The Doctor is often referred to by number, accordingly Tom Baker's portrayal of The Doctor from 1974 to 1981 is referred to as the Fourth Doctor and Peter Capaldi's portrayal from 2014 to 2017 is referred to as the Twelfth Doctor. In late 2023, viewers will be introduced to the Fifteenth Doctor (Ncuti Gatwa) of the series. The Doctor is presented predominantly as male, but the Thirteenth Doctor (Jodie Whittaker) and The Fugitive Doctor (Jo Martin) are female. Consequently, in this book when referring to specific Doctors, I will use male pronouns where appropriate and female pronouns where appropriate, although the personal pronouns of their and they are used most frequently when discussing The Doctors as a whole.

The Doctor's Companions are a wonderful mix of characters with distinct personalities, skills, backgrounds, and aptitudes. What unites them is their commitment to The Doctor, sense of adventure and their capacity to take risks. As their relationship with The Doctor deepens, they develop their followership behaviors and demonstrate courageous followership in achieving successful resolutions to the conflicts and dilemmas they face in their travels, as well as being able to moderate The Doctor's excesses and destructive behaviors. For the most part, I will write about those companions who properly travel with The Doctor, but there will be other followers who are important examples of courageousness, such as Wilfred Mott, Harriet Jones, and The Osgoods. A brief description of the Companions and other characters mentioned in this book can be found in Appendix 1.

I am also limiting my discussion of *Doctor Who* to the series from 2005 to 2022. My reasoning for this is because… well, 203 episodes is more than enough to discuss followership and adding the 695 episodes of *Classic Doctor Who* into the analysis is not quite feasible for the time and space I occupy, and I do not possess a TARDIS to make it easier.

ORGANIZATION OF THIS BOOK

Throughout this book, I will be discussing followership, leadership, and provide examples of these concepts and theories from *Doctor Who*, as well as posing questions for reflection to readers to help develop their skills as courageous followers. Familiarity with *Doctor Who* (2005–2022) or Chaleff's (2009) book is not essential but may be helpful. The series is available to stream or purchase through several services and the book is widely available in several formats. For an even deeper dive, there are numerous *Doctor Who* fan sites, significant information about the series on IMDb and Wikipedia, and Chaleff also has a wonderful website devoted to courageous followership.

In Chapter 1, I examine the courage to engage in personal growth as a purposeful start to becoming a courageous follower. Emotional intelligence skills are a key contributor to successful relationships and followers can gain important advantages by developing their self-awareness, self-management, empathy, and social skills. Another factor for personal growth is being able to overcome resistance to change. The ability to reflect upon why one is averse to change and how that can harm their professional and personal progress is a significant part of defeating fears and being open to new experiences in collaboration with others.

Chapter 2 discusses the importance of taking responsibility as a follower and not being passive or merely present. Courageous followers must find the internal motivation to ignite their passion to achieve the goals and take the initiative. In addition, ensuring one's personal values connect to the organization's cultural norms provides a path toward taking responsibility and the initiative in a positive manner. However, sometimes it is important to break the rules.

Service to the leader, others, and the mission requires significant amounts of courage. Chapter 3 speaks the importance of serving with courage through trust and open communication. Equally important are being conscientious about the time and attention needed from the leader, being able to defend the leader from detractors without anger or dismissing a leader's flaws, as well as tending to the physical or emotional needs of the leader when they may be ill.

Chapter 4 explores the need for courage when challenging the leader by combatting their self-deception and providing clear and candid feedback. Followers can challenge directly, but there are also indirect ways in which to challenge leaders that may prove more successful depending on the situation.

In Chapter 5, I discuss the role of followers in creating change and transformation. Resistance to change is discussed more fully and the function of followers as change agents. Coping with transformation can be exceedingly difficult for followers, and a discussion of the stages of grief and renewal followers pass through in their journey of accepting transformation is examined.

Sometimes, it is simply inevitable that followers must part ways with their leaders or organizations. Chapter 6 explores how followers can part ways with courage whether they must disobey, withdraw their support, or place their energies and values in other places. Notably, it also takes courage to stay.

Chapter 7 moves to the concepts of enriching behaviors that leaders and courageous followers engage in to be effective and meet their objectives. Challenging the hierarchy is an important responsibility for leaders and followers, whether it is communicating information, educating the hierarchy, or speaking the truth to power. In addition, leaders must be open to the efforts of their followers and be accepting of support and input.

In Chapter 8, I move away from the Chaleff model of courageous followership and offer three principles for effective followership. Love, forgiveness, and redemption are themes found in the *Doctor Who* series which directly connect to the ways in which The Doctor and Companions co-construct the leadership process. For both leaders and followers, each of these principles requires a certain amount of courage in building and maintaining their interpersonal relationship and ability to achieve common goals.

Chapter 9 provides a summary of the book and suggestions as to how readers can use this newfound knowledge to develop their own courage and followership behaviors in the real world.

There are numerous characters in the *Doctor Who* series who are important to our understanding of courageous followership. I have included Appendix 1 which is a listing of the characters discussed in this book with a brief description to help readers who may not be familiar with the series or need a refresher for recalling different characters. Appendix 2 is an episode guide of each episode discussed in the book for quick reference if you want to research the episode more fully. Readers will also find a reference list that may prove useful for further reading on the topics in this book.

1

COURAGE FOR PERSONAL GROWTH

Being a follower to an impulsive arrogant leader isn't easy – especially if that leader is an alien Time Lord with a time machine who has lived for millennia and doesn't really like to talk about the past or even share their name. It would be quite acceptable to politely walk away after an adventure running from Daleks or combatting Cybermen and be thankful to be alive. But what we find in *Doctor Who* is a series of followers who decide to continue traveling with The Doctor even though they know the risks are extreme and can include death. As Rose Tyler tells her mother and boyfriend, "The Doctor showed me a better way to live my life" (*The Parting of the Ways*, 2005). These Companions make the choice to be courageous in their growth and development of who they are as people. The courage for personal growth is an essential characteristic to be a valuable follower.

Ancient Greek philosophers considered courage to be the overcoming of fear, particularly on the battlefield (Kateb, 2004). Courage is considered a virtue, even though there is nothing very virtuous about acts of war where death and destruction are the objective. However, overcoming fear remains a strong virtue for personal development. As Clara Oswald tells a young Doctor in *Listen* (2014), "You're always going to be afraid, even if you learn to hide it." It takes courage to identify one's fears and take action to overcome them. It takes courage to be vulnerable and acknowledge one's limitations while striving to be better and contribute in many ways. It takes courage to stand up to the powerful and advocate for change. Knowing oneself is a key to being able to develop future relationships with others and reaching shared goals. This is the courageous process of personal growth and development.

PERSONAL GROWTH AND EMOTIONAL INTELLIGENCE

One area that requires a certain amount of courage and allows followers to develop as individuals and deepen their relationship with their leaders is to cultivate their emotional intelligence skills. Typically, emotional intelligence is discussed as something that leaders need to nurture. But if we want to think about followers and leaders as partners, who are interdependent and mutually benefit from their relationship, it's important to understand emotional intelligence needs to be developed in followers as well.

Daniel Goleman (2014) sets out four components of emotional intelligence: self-awareness, self-management, empathy, and social skill. Self-awareness is knowing our own strengths, weaknesses, needs, triggers, and drives. Self-aware people are deeply mindful of their own values and their goals, and they act in ways that are aligned to those values. There is a need for courage in not only being aware of oneself, but the Companions must also have the courage to resist acting in ways that violate their values.

In *The Beast Below* (2010), the eleventh Doctor and Amy Pond travel to the colony ship, Starship UK. This is Amy's first adventure with The Doctor into the future and off planet Earth. The ship they teleport to, sits on the back of a star whale and, is powered through the vastness of space by inducing horrific pain in the star whale's brain. Star whales are extremely rare, and this may be one of the last of its kind in the universe. When Amy is made aware of the torture and the dire consequences for the British survivors of Earth's destruction, if the star whale is freed from the cruelty, she chooses to protect the humans and pushes a button that allows her to forget the truth. Amy understands she doesn't have the strength to reconcile the competing needs of human survival and the immorality of torturing animals. It is a trigger she doesn't want to face.

Later, Queen Elizabeth X, known as Liz 10, must also face the situation of either forgetting she condones the torture of rare animals to protect her people and ensure their survival or abdicate the throne and the star whale will be freed with the possibility that it may leave the colony stranded in the void of space. The Doctor is reluctantly about to give the star whale a lobotomy so that it will still respond to the electrical pulses causing it to move forward, but the beast will be unable to register the pain.

This time, Amy finds her courage to act in alignment with her values and the deeper values of those around her. She remembers seeing the star whale is sympathetic to the crying of children and bonds with them more than older humans as she misses her own children. The star whale actually volunteered to take the British colony ship into space to find a new home because she could not abide the sound of crying children. Amy grabs the monarch's hand forcing Liz 10 to hit the abdicate button. The torture stops and the star whale begins to speed up. Amy remarks, "Yeah, well when you stop torturing the pilot" (*The Beast Below*, 2010).

Amy's self-awareness of her inability to accept the horror of what was happening to the star whale against what might happen to humans meant she was unable to align her values and actions in the first instance of confronting the truth about the starship. However, she was able to grow in her understanding of her own strengths, values, and goals to seek out a resolution to these competing values by being attentive to the situation around her. She courageously acted without permission against those with higher authority in a manner that set actions and values in alignment, even though she risked a dreadful outcome for everyone.

The second component of emotional intelligence is self-management, which allows people to control their emotions (Goleman, 2014). This doesn't mean we should be stoic and emotionless but be able to use our emotions in constructive ways. Self-management prevents impulsive behaviors and encourages reflection so that we can act with integrity and make better decisions, especially in stressful situations. Self-management is also a motivating attribute as we can use our positive emotions to push us toward our goals.

In 1914, Martha Jones is compelled to keep her emotions in check when she is working as a servant in a school for privileged boys and must endure overt racism and misogyny. She courageously fulfills her duty in protecting the Tenth Doctor who is in hiding and does not know his real identity or hers. Additionally, she watches The Doctor fall in love with a woman who is not her, which is very hurtful though she can't let him or anyone else know her feelings for him. She could easily give up, but she stays positive and motivated toward the ensuring the safety and eventual return of The Doctor (*Human Nature*, 2007; *The Family Blood*, 2007).

When Donna Noble first meets the Tenth Doctor in *The Runaway Bride* (2006), her emotions spill out constantly in every direction. She is angry she has been abducted from the altar on her wedding day. She is fearful of the robots disguised as Santa that are trying to kill her. She is intensely annoyed that The Doctor is not able to help her in the way she wants. All these emotions she throws at The Doctor, and, to his credit, he generally takes it in stride, though he is just as bewildered at the situation. Her ability to manage her emotions is practically nonexistent when they first meet.

The next time they meet, in *Partners in Crime* (2008), it's Donna's turn to manage her emotions while the Tenth Doctor is frantic. He is trying to hack a computer and prevent the death of a million people from the parasitic adipose ready to burst from their human hosts. Donna asks what he needs, but he is dismissive. She calmly asks again, and he irritably snaps that he needs another adipose capsule to boost the energy. She shows him the capsule she has, and they are able to stop the adipose from breaking through. Without her ability to stay focused and engaged in helping The Doctor while keeping her emotions under control, many people would have died, and the adipose babies could have been in danger as well. Nevertheless, what makes Donna an amazing and courageous companion for The Doctor is her gift for being in touch with her emotions and able to experience and express them in appropriate ways.

Another example of a companion being able to manage and use their emotions in appropriate ways is when Bill Potts has been transformed into a Cyberman (*World Enough and Time*, 2017). Even though Bill has been surgically "upgraded," she holds onto her self-awareness. She experiences all the emotions of her human self in the years she spends waiting for the Eleventh Doctor to find her. Accessing these emotions and using them in her interactions with those who have her captive allows her to maintain her humanity and not succumb to the emotionless state typical of Cybermen.

Indeed, even after she has finally discovered she appears as a Cyberman, she is asked by The Doctor and other humans to stay calm as heated emotions can have dire consequences, such as inadvertently shooting laser beams from her headgear that destroy the doors of a barn. An important moment in the personal growth of Bill Potts and one demonstration of her courage is when she is asked to use her anger and hurt to fight against the other Cybermen as they attack. She is not only able to manage her intense emotions in useful ways to meet the immediate goals but also show her commitment and humanity to the group (*The Doctor Falls*, 2017). Her courage in following The Doctor and remaining committed to their purpose and mission does not diminish simply because she is in a cyberbody, in fact it heightens our empathy and understanding of her courage in facing the fear of not being accepted for whom she is beneath the outward trappings of a Cyberman.

Empathy is our ability to consider the needs and feelings of others when making decisions (Goleman, 2014). It goes beyond the simplistic notion of "putting yourself in someone else's shoes." Brené Brown (2018) explains empathy as a vulnerable choice to connect to others' emotions not just their experiences. It takes courage to open ourselves to someone else's emotions because we must experience our own emotions in the process. Empathy is also about perspective taking and considering viewpoints outside of our experience without judgment. For the Companions, their courage to develop their empathy often places them in direct conflict with The Doctor's decisions. For example, in *The Fires of Pompeii* (2008) Donna Noble desperately tries to convince the Tenth Doctor to warn the people of Pompeii, they must evacuate as Mount Vesuvius is erupting. Her empathy for the people and their impending death puts her in direct conflict with the Tenth Doctor who insists he can do nothing because it is a fixed moment in time and cannot be changed. Ultimately, she influences the Tenth Doctor to save one family and this change in The Doctor's empathetic capabilities foreshadows a significant journey of growth for The Doctor in his twelfth regeneration.

In many ways, Donna Noble's time as a Companion serves to not only build her own emotional intelligence skills but to help the Tenth Doctor build his empathy. Her empathetic influence becomes an important skill set in the co-construction of the leadership process as it complements the jaded and tamped down emotional reactions of The Doctor. In addition to the example above, Donna stops the Tenth Doctor from uncontrolled destruction against the Racnoss in *The Runaway Bride* (2008) due to her empathy for the lives of the Empress Racnoss' children. She is pleased The Doctor won't blow up the spaceship that serves as a nursery for the adipose babies in *Partners in Crime* (2008) and tells him he has changed since their experience with the Racnoss. In *Planet of the Ood* (2008), Donna's intense empathy with the oppressed and enslaved Ood helps her influence The Doctor to help liberate them. At the end of their adventures together, the Tenth Doctor has indeed increased his empathetic abilities and is not as quick to use his substantial skills to over-power or dismiss others. The courage Donna displays in developing her own empathy and then helping The Doctor develop theirs is critical to the development of their overall leader–follower relationship. The Doctor is still a bit socially awkward but learns to appropriately respond to others with empathy, sometimes using flashcards (see *Under the Lake*, 2015; *Face the Raven*, 2015), but the ability to understand they need to access the flashcards is a big step.

The final component of Goleman's (2014) emotional intelligence model is social skill. This attribute is not simply being friendly or knowing a lot of people but understanding the dynamics of relationships that bring about the achievement of goals. People who have strong social skills recognize "nothing important gets done alone" (Goleman, 2014, p. 17) and cultivate networks of others who are ready to act when the time comes. The Doctor may prefer to act alone due to the fear of losing a companion or their own hubris, but Companions know the importance of working as a team and leverage their relationships with courage to act together, especially in the absence of The Doctor.

The ultimate example of Companions being ready to act together in fulfilling their purpose of defeating the Daleks and defending the Earth comes in the two-part storyline of *The Stolen Earth* (2008) and *Journey's End* (2008). Former Prime Minister Harriet Jones pulls together a team of Companions, Martha Jones, Sarah Jane Smith, and the Torchwood Team of Captain Jack Harkness, Gwen Cooper, and Ianto Jones, to fight against the Daleks who have stolen the Earth and teleported it to a distant part of the universe known as the Medusa Cascade. Rose Tyler has returned from the parallel universe and is a part of the effort but cannot communicate with the others on their sub-wave network due to a faulty webcam. Jackie Tyler and Mickey Smith also arrive from the other universe to help in the effort. The Tenth Doctor and Donna Noble are far away with the Shadow Proclamation, the galactic police authority, trying to locate Earth.

Harriet Jones has prepared the sub-wave network and defense plan for the time when The Doctor is not there to save them, and they must rely on their own abilities as they await The Doctor's arrival. With Harriet Jones' no-nonsense leadership, the team of Companions work together to boost a signal that can bypass the Daleks and message The Doctor to let him know Earth is in trouble and where they are located. The former Prime Minister sacrifices her own life to Dalek invaders to fulfill her mission to defend Earth. After The Doctor arrives and the Daleks are defeated, the entire group of Companions work together flying the TARDIS as it tows the Earth back to its proper place in the universe. The Companions clearly understand the important dynamics of networking and sharing tasks to reach a goal, but more importantly they are seen enjoying the company of each other and building even stronger relationships with each other. No one appears to consider themselves any less important than the others, though Jackie is comically not offered the opportunity to help fly the TARDIS. Essentially, the Companions reflect the concept that "nothing gets done alone" and depend on the unique skills and abilities of each other to reach their objective.

Emotional intelligence is a relatively straightforward concept for personal growth but isn't simplistic or uncomplicated. The act of reflecting to become more self-aware, improve the management of our emotions, have true empathy for others, and build strong relationships can be difficult for many of us. In our busy lives we don't always take the time to be mindful and circumspect about ourselves and our actions. We worry over our failures to act in emotionally intelligent ways instead of looking at how we are successful. We challenge ourselves to change the ways we have been feeling and behaving, yet forget to give ourselves the time and grace it takes to accomplish the transformation. Through the Companions we see how being courageous in our personal growth is not necessarily linear, but a process that ebbs and flows.

PERSONAL GROWTH AND RESISTANCE TO CHANGE

Personal growth is about change and that can be a scary prospect. Conventional wisdom tells us people don't like change in their lives, though people will get married, have children, go to graduate school, or retire from the workforce, which are all very big changes. Ultimately, the ambiguity about the outcomes of change or the sense of powerlessness against changes is what many people fear. When we don't know what will happen on the other side of a change or don't want to put in the considerable effort to create changes, we reject the change and try to hold onto the status quo for as long as we can. We'll explore the idea of resistance to change in more detail in Chapter 5. For now, it's important to understand we need to muster the courage to set aside our fears about the future and seek to create the positive results we desire even if it's hard.

When the Companions decide to travel with The Doctor, each of them makes a decision that upsets the status quo of their lives and offers opportunities for personal growth. While their first adventure is typically unexpected, such as when Donna Noble is whooshed away from her wedding to inside the TARDIS (*The Runaway Bride*, 2006) or when Rory's dad Brian is inadvertently included in *Dinosaurs on a Spaceship* (2012), choices are made to continue their journey of personal growth. Even so, the advantages can be dubious, as Captain Jack Harkness tells the Ninth Doctor as he goes off to fight the dreaded Daleks, "I wish I had never met you. I was much better off as a coward" (*The Parting of the Ways*, 2005).

Chaleff (2009) explains personal growth can be very uncomfortable as it demands we look at ourselves critically and see the darker unattractive sides of who we are. Yet, if followers are to be able to transform their leaders and pull them away from the dark side of autocracy, they must know the whereabouts of the abyss. It's emotionally challenging and does require the courage to mindfully consider our own weaknesses, biases, self-serving attitudes, and sometimes the desire to just give up and walk away. But for the courageous follower, they forge ahead with the knowledge that being uncomfortable is a sign of personal growth and by seeking out challenges they will continue to accept responsibility for their growth.

There are numerous examples of the Companions coming to terms with being uncomfortable and meeting that challenge with courage. Rose Tyler's first adventure in space with the Ninth Doctor brings her into contact with a variety of life forms and she is rather uneasy in their presence but puts aside her prejudices and persists in helping The Doctor and others root out the life-form that is attacking the space station (*End of the World*, 2005). Even though Donna Noble ultimately helps to liberate the Ood, her first reaction was the desire to go home because traveling with The Doctor was not as wonderful as she imagined. Nevertheless, she didn't give up and develops her personal qualities to become an important complement to The Doctor (*Planet of the Ood*, 2008). While Graham O'Brien is an atypical older Companion and has just overcome a bout of cancer and the death of his wife, he chooses to challenge himself not to be set in his ways and travel with the Thirteenth Doctor (*Arachnids in the UK*, 2018).

SUMMARY

In this chapter, we discussed personal growth as a means by which followers can be courageous and help leaders. Followers overcome their fears and challenge themselves to develop personal attributes of self-awareness, self-management, empathy, and social skills which are collectively known as emotional intelligence. People who possess strong emotional intelligence skills understand their strengths, limitations, and desires. They can articulate personal values and align their actions to their values. They are able to manage their emotions in constructive ways. They engage in perspective taking and consider others' feelings. Emotionally intelligent people also recognize the importance of teamwork and building relationships with others to achieve goals. When followers act with the courage to grow, it can sometimes lead to conflict and emotional challenges. The lessons to be learned from self-reflection and emotional challenges far outweigh the fleeting feelings of discomfort.

REFLECTIVE ACTIVITIES

- To develop your own courage to grow, consider what personal develop-ment activities would be beneficial for you. If you are not familiar with emotional intelligence and would like to build those skills, reflect on your strengths, what motivates you, your values, and the way in which you are able to constructively use your emotions. Find opportunities to actively listen to others and share an emotional connection without judging or trying to solve their problem. Look for occasions that help you build bonds with others through shared purpose or experience. Reflect on the ways in which you intentionally align your values to your actions. Don't forget to think about how uncomfortable you feel and how you can use those feelings as learning opportunities.

- Resistance to change is often an obstacle to personal growth, as well as organizational success. Think about how susceptible you are to main-taining the status quo in your personal life or in your professional life and how that prevents growth and success. Do you see change as an opportunity or a threat? Be mindful of the small moments that pop up when you could take a chance and do something differently and have a successful experience. Then reflect on your emotions in that moment. Were you practicing self-awareness and self-management? Did it require you to be empathetic or develop a relationship to complete an objective? What could you do in the future to help you drive change behaviors?

- Some readers may be familiar with SWOT analyses. SWOT stands for Strengths, Weaknesses, Opportunities, and Threats. As an exercise, take a piece of paper and draw four quadrants labeling the top left Strengths, the top right Weaknesses, the bottom left Opportunities, and the bottom right Threats. Now, consider an item you would like to work on in your personal growth and development. Maybe, it's being open to new experiences or building stronger relationships. In each quadrant, make a short list corresponding to the SWOT category. What is a strength to help you in your development? What is a threat to your development? Some of you may find duplicates in the quadrants and that's okay – pay attention to those! Sometimes, you will find a strength can also be a weakness and a threat can also be an opportunity. Once you have finished, review your SWOT analysis, and reflect on how you can use this information to move forward in your personal development actions by exercising your strengths, taking advantage of your opportunities, improving upon your weaknesses, and limiting your threats.

2

COURAGEOUS RESPONSIBILITY

When considering the co-construction of the leadership process between followers and leaders through the ideal of developing the relationship between them into a mature partnership characterized by mutual trust, respect, and obligations, having the courage to take responsibility becomes central to the success of their dyadic relationship. For followers to support their leaders, they employ their courage to be passionate, take initiative, stay true to their values, contribute over complaining, and sometimes break the rules (Chaleff, 2009).

IGNITING PASSION

As Chaleff (2009) explains, being enthusiastic about something means we are connected to the mission and purpose of what we are doing. We care deeply about the outcomes and know we have a unique role to play in succeeding. We take ownership of our time and space in reaching shared goals. Yet there are times when we can feel our passion receding. For these times, we must be courageous and ask ourselves tough questions as to why we are losing our passion. Do we feel disconnected from the mission? Are our interpersonal relationships with the leader or team becoming difficult? Are we experiencing boredom and need additional or greater responsibilities? Perhaps we feel overwhelmed and not capable of fulfilling our current obligations. By reigniting our passion, we reconnect with our power to help shape the future (Chaleff, 2009).

Amy Pond and Rory Williams question their continuing passion for traveling with the Eleventh Doctor and their neglect of home and work (*The Power of Three*, 2012). They solve a mystery of cubes that suddenly appeared on Earth and their ability to solve that mystery and once again defend the Earth reignites their passion for the journey as they cleverly understand it takes the power of the three of them to be successful.

Although Martha Jones nearly died when the hospital where she worked was taken to the moon by a galactic goon squad known as the Judoon (*Smith and Jones*, 2007), her passion for traveling with the Tenth Doctor was reignited when they went to Elizabethan England and met William Shakespeare (*The Shakespeare Code*, 2007). As The Doctor takes her home after several other adventures involving The Face of Boa in the far future (*Gridlock*, 2007) and Daleks in 1930s New York City (*Daleks in Manhattan*, 2007), she is a bit concerned and depressed her journey with him may be over. She has developed a crush on him, though he doesn't reciprocate. But The Doctor comes right back – which is unusual – and they have another adventure on Earth where Martha has the opportunity to offer her medical knowledge and skills as a complement to The Doctor's abilities (*The Lazarus Experiment*, 2007). In each of these adventures, Martha discovers her power in helping to shape the future and builds her ability to take courageous responsibility for continuing the mission and purpose of The Doctor in defending the Earth.

TAKING INITIATIVE

When followers recognize their passion for the purpose – and how it sometimes may take precedent over their commitment to the leader – the conditions are ideal for courageous followers to assume even greater responsibility and take initiative to act without specific direction from the leader. Followers who have a keen sense of their own intrinsic motivation and role as a collaborative partner in the leadership process are more likely to demonstrate autonomy in decision-making and act (Vondey, 2008). Leaders can be agreeable to follower initiatives if they know followers are acting on behalf of the mission and not just for their own ambitions. This does require that leaders maintain open honest communications and followers must be certain they have all the facts for their decision-making as the opposite can also be true. "It is a failure of responsibility to act when the risks are unacceptable and acting endangers the organization's purpose or violates its values" (Chaleff, 2009, p. 49).

There are numerous events in the series where Companions have the courage to accept responsibility and take initiatives to act in ways that further the mission and purpose. Rose Tyler looks into the heart of the TARDIS and is able to disintegrate the entire Dalek fleet and save The Doctor and Captain Jack Harkness (*The Parting of the Ways*, 2005). Martha Jones courageously travels across the globe spreading the story of The Doctor in anticipation of being free from the tyranny of The Master (*Last of the Time Lords*, 2007). In the time after her cancelled wedding, Donna Noble has been investigating and cataloging all the odd happenings on Earth in furtherance of defending Earth, which brings her to the Adipose Company and meeting The Doctor again (*Partners in Crime*, 2008). Yasmin Khan and Dan Lewis also travel for years around Earth using tunnels under Liverpool to jump between time streams as they try to find the date for the world's end (*Survivors of the Flux*, 2021; *The Vanquishers*, 2021).

But in *The Christmas Invasion* (2005), we see how the actions of a courageous follower can undermine the relationship with The Doctor. In this episode, Prime Minister Harriet Jones broadcasts a plea for The Doctor to help save Earth from an invasion of the Sycorax. They have a strong relationship from their previous encounter, but as the Tenth Doctor has just regenerated, it is slightly different and awkward. After the Tenth Doctor is victorious in a sword match with the leader of the Sycorax, he allows them to leave, but banishes them from returning to Earth. The planet has been saved once again, though the Tenth Doctor tells PM Jones there are many other alien species who may be looking to conquer Earth. Jones takes the initiative to have the Sycorax spaceship destroyed so no other species will inadvertently gain knowledge of planet Earth. The Tenth Doctor is furious and accuses her of murder and being a monster, but the PM counters that it was justified defensive action as The Doctor is not always there to defend them. In retaliation, he begins a whisper campaign alleging false health concerns. Jones ultimately loses her position as PM.

In this episode, we see how The Doctor and PM Jones demonstrate a failure in the leader–follower relationship involving shared purpose and values. They begin as collaborative partners in the leadership process to influence others toward ridding Earth of alien occupiers, but their primary purposes and values are different and culminate in actions by the other they deem dangerous and irresponsible. The risk of other aliens finding Earth is unacceptable to the PM and, from her perspective, she acts responsibly to uphold her primary purpose and value to protect the planet and its people by having the ship destroyed. The Tenth Doctor considers her actions in destroying the ship to be unconscionable and holds a different perspective where his purpose is to be the sole savior of the planet and resolve differences without wholesale slaughter and his words to the Sycorax guaranteeing their safety are of great value to him. His petty rumormongering demonstrates his belief that Jones acted selfishly to maintain her power and he has decided to exercise his own power and take away her legitimate authority.

CONNECTING CULTURAL NORMS TO VALUES

It's difficult to stay true to our values in the face of an organizational culture that may be undergoing transformation. Our survival instinct may lead us into behaving with cultural norms that contrast with our personal values. Typically, followers uphold traditions and norms to maintain cohesion and build synergy. If our values do not align with an organization, it's acceptable to leave the organization, but a courageous follower will find respectful ways to role model other behaviors that could bring the organization greater effectiveness, diversity of perspectives, and integrity (Chaleff, 2009).

The Osgoods, scientific advisors to Unified Intelligence Taskforce (UNIT), exemplify this through their Operation Duplicate. They are identical beings, but one of them is human and the other is a Zygon shape shifter taking the appearance of a human. The Zygons are refugees on Earth and shape shift as humans to live their lives in peace and harmony. While UNIT and much of the human race is intolerant of alien lifeforms, it would be understandable if The Osgoods chose to leave UNIT and publicly denounced the bigotry and prejudice humans hold for Others. But The Osgoods choose to role model behaviors of tolerance and persist in their job to make UNIT more effective and provide diverse perspectives to the ever-present threats to Earth. They defend Earth not through attacking alien lifeforms, but by living in harmony and acceptance of Otherness. They defend the values of the Earth through the courage of their commitment to keeping their nature as human or Zygon noncommittal, which results in the questioning of the necessity in labeling any beings (*The Zygon Invasion*, 2015; *The Zygon Inversion*, 2015).

BREAKING THE RULES

When assuming courageous responsibility, followers not only influence the culture by upholding or challenging group norms, but they also find ways to break the rules in service to the greater purpose. As adults, our relationship to rules enables us to "support rules when they serve the common purpose and question rules when they thwart the purpose" (Chaleff, 2009, p. 51). Rules are guidelines and, as we know from observing The Doctor, rules aren't really that important. Even time can be a bit "wibbly-wobbly timey-wimey" (*Blink*, 2007) and not the linear experience we mere humans consider an inviolate rule.

What is important is follower attitudes toward rules and how those attitudes can affect the leader–follower relationship. For example, while follower types who are passive or compliant may follow orders without question, courageous followers won't follow rules that are unethical or disrespect basic human decency. Other follower types, such as Kellerman's (2007) bystanders, might complain about the rules, but a courageous follower contributes to overcoming the obstacles and creating rules that meet organizational needs. A courageous follower will recognize when rules run counter to achieving goals and find ways to bypass those rules and get the job done. Notably, courageous followers don't do this in secret. They are open about their actions and ready to defend what they did with faithfulness to the leader and organizational purpose (Chaleff, 2009).

Sometimes, leaders, peers, or organizations aren't ready to change the rules and find new ways of doing things that can be more efficient, effective, or just. In these cases, courageous followers undertake the responsibility to test new ideas through demonstrating their effectiveness and value to the organization and others. These initiatives allow courageous followers to build support and consensus for change, instead of simply shrugging in the face of impediments and complications (Chaleff, 2009).

Rose Tyler breaks several rules as she continues her faithfulness to The Doctor and the overriding purpose of defending the Earth. She opens the heart of the TARDIS and stares into the time vortex, which enables her to destroy the Dalek fleet and make Captain Jack Harkness immortal (*The Parting of the Ways*, 2005). She travels back and forth between parallel universes in *Partners in Crime* (2008) and *Turn Left* (2008) looking for The Doctor and risking damage to the space–time continuum, as well as potentially causing Donna Noble's death.

Clara Oswald breaks the rules almost by the definition of her existence. As "the impossible girl," she discovers there is a memory of her that has traveled through all of space and time to watch over The Doctor and help him to stay on the proper path (*The Name of the Doctor*, 2013). In *The Asylum of the Daleks* (2012), an argument can be made that she is still the impossible girl, but in Dalek form, as she helps the Eleventh Doctor, Amy, and Rory escape the asylum and wipes all memories of The Doctor from the Daleks. She even tells The Doctor, "Run you clever boy, and remember" (*Asylum of the Daleks*, 2012). Clara also returns as a barmaid and governess in *The Snowmen* (2012) who dies at the hand of The Great Intelligence but motivates The Doctor to discover who she is and why he keeps meeting her. Clara breaks the ultimate rule of existence by refusing to return to Gallifrey and resume her place in history where she will die within her next heartbeat. Instead, she flies off with Ashildr/Me in a TARDIS that looks like an old-fashioned American diner to "take the long way around" and serve the mission and purpose of defending others across the universe (*Hell Bent*, 2015).

Breaking rules is not an action to simply be destructive or contrary. To break the rules with courage, one must know there is not another option for fulfilling the purpose or upholding personal values. It's acceptable to question the rules and the status quo, as well as to break them, as long as one is willing to assume responsibility and act with courage to serve the greater purpose.

SUMMARY

In this chapter, we discovered how courageous followers take responsibility for achieving goals by understanding how their values connect with organizational mission and purpose and their behaviors role model passion, initiative to act, adherence to cultural norms or transforming norms for the better, and breaking rules when necessary. Courageous followers have a strong sense of self-motivation, and viewing themselves as collaborative partners with their leader allows them to have greater autonomy and decision-making capabilities.

REFLECTIVE ACTIVITIES

- How passionate are you about the organization where you work, volunteer, or study? If you are strongly connected, how might you use your passion to improve the organization or reach goals more effectively? If you aren't as passionate as you would like to be, what is the root cause of your dissatisfaction? What courageous steps will you take to reignite your passion?

- How comfortable are you to take the initiative at your workplace, school, or community to achieve goals or create change? What might be holding you back and what steps can you take to increase your courage to assume responsibility and act?

- Consider an organization you belong to where you believe the rules to be stringent or unfair. Reflect on why these rules are in place. Do they allow employees or customers to have a safe environment free from physical or emotional harm? Do they prevent unethical or illegal behaviors? Do the rules connect to the mission, purpose, and values the organization espouses? What is the level of effectiveness of the rules? What rules would you change and what courageous acts would you employ to bring about change?

3

SERVING WITH COURAGE

Serving the leader with courage is not to be confused with being servile. Leaders want followers to accept more responsibility and initiate ideas and take actions, which is the way their dyadic relationship develops, so they can serve each other and the organization. The courageous follower will serve by unburdening the leader and make decisions in their stead, if not in their name. In addition, courageous followers don't insist on excessive access. Their relationship is robust enough for each to understand how the other thinks or feels and make decisions accordingly. Serving with courage also means taking care of the leader's physical or mental health. Reminding them to slow down, take a break, or open up about what is bothering them are all actions courageous followers can take to show their concern for the leader's well-being. These can be difficult and delicate conversations, so the level of mutual trust must be strong. While leaders acknowledge their role in serving their followers, courageous followers understand their role in taking care of their leaders is a partnership of mutual service to each other and shared goals (Chaleff, 2009).

THE IMPORTANCE OF TRUST

Many of us know leaders who believe they are responsible for every day-to-day detail and only they can fix a problem. Perhaps you or someone you know adheres to the thinking of "If I want something done right, I need to do it myself" because they simply don't trust anyone. This type of leader is dangerously close to autocratic behaviors that could harm a group or organization. Their lack of trust impedes the ability of the organization to develop strong employees and succession plans. Moreover, they are behaving more like managers dealing with the complexity of daily tasks rather than leaders concentrating on the future vision and overall strategy. Leaders who do not delegate tasks or train and empower others to solve problems are highly ineffective and placing too much stress upon themselves for reaching goals. Due to their lack of trust, they run the risk of alienating their followers and creating a culture of minimum effort and dependency. They may be the ones who find themselves inundated with trivial questions and decisions to be made, which is the classic example of "putting out fires all day." Indeed, their self-identity as leaders may be at risk because they are neglecting the role followers play in the creation of leadership identities and their internal motivation to continue as a leader could be jeopardized (Jiang et al., 2021). Their heroic idealization of leadership will cause them to simply burnout. A courageous follower will disabuse these leaders of those notions and demonstrate how they can be of service to the leader and the organization. Courageous followers find ways to build trust with the leader.

Unfortunately, The Doctor does not give their trust easily, even though they want their Companions to trust them. Many of the Companions say they trust The Doctor with their life, including River Song, Rose Tyler, Jack Harkness, and others. But there always seems to be a bit of a risk about whether that trust should be placed. Amy Pond tells the Eleventh Doctor it is hard to trust him when he doesn't always tell her the truth (*The Time of Angels*, 2010).

Still, Companions work toward earning trust and enabling The Doctor to trust them to do the right thing, solve problems, and be helpful. The Twelfth Doctor says he trusts Clara Oswald as he abandons her to the half-face cyborg. But her trust in The Doctor is not very high as she is struggling with acceptance of the Twelfth Doctor who has just regenerated. In a moment where she might very well die, she reminds herself of the trust she has built with the Eleventh Doctor. As she slowly reaches her arm behind her, she whispers, "that no matter what, The Doctor will always have my back" (*Deep Breath*, 2014). And he does.

For the Thirteenth Doctor, we find she does trust her Companions fully enough to delegate tasks. She sends Yasmin Khan, Graham O'Brien, and Ryan Sinclair off on their own investigative errands when they are trying to discover the cause of a deadly bacterium in *Praxeus* (2020). This has previously not been the norm, however, and Companions often need to courageously speak up and remind The Doctor of their trustworthiness.

Building trust is crucial to developing the interpersonal relationship between a leader and follower, and helping to move the relationship along the path from Stranger to Acquaintance to Partner. Sometimes building trust is an act of faith, such as what Clara displayed with the Twelfth Doctor, but it can also be accepting the trust from a leader, such as the example of the Thirteenth Doctor's Companions.

WILLINGNESS TO COMMUNICATE

When followers are courageous enough to co-construct the leadership process by building trust with a leader who may initially lack the ability or will to trust them, this also demonstrates how followers perceive themselves as able to solve problems. When followers feel empowered and capable of problem-solving and decision-making within the dyadic leadership relationship, they also find themselves more willing to communicate to leaders, offer suggestions and alternatives, and express themselves to the leader (Inderjeet & Scheepers, 2022).

Nevertheless, courageous followers need to follow a few guidelines for effective communication, such as making sure they have high-value communications that don't ramble or get too far into the weeds. They should also be certain to communicate through the methods the leader prefers (Chaleff, 2009). For Rose Tyler, Martha Jones, and Clara Oswald, this includes using the quaint 21st Century technology of personal mobile phones to both contact The Doctor and have them contact her. But for River Song, she leaves messages across time and space – sometimes with the message "Hello, sweetie" to verify it is her. She embeds a message on the ancient flight recorder of a starship with space coordinates so the Eleventh Doctor can catch her with the TARDIS as she ejects from the exploding starship (*The Time of Angels*, 2010) and writes a pulp detective novel under the pseudonym Melody Malone the Eleventh Doctor reads in contemporary time and gains clues as to the troubling problems in 1930's New York City with Weeping Angels (*The Angels Take Manhattan*, 2012). She even defaces an ancient monument by changing the unreadable glyphs into a message (*The Pandorica Opens*, 2010).

When serving with courage to solve problems, followers must be willing to not only communicate options, but also consider whether they actually know enough to offer advice, as it can be a fine line between facts, intuition, and just wanting to please the leader. We want to be supportive of our leaders, but we should never exaggerate our knowledge or even our confidence in sharing options for problem-solving. Again, the situation requires trust and the self-assurance that our relationship with our leader is mature enough to withstand our honesty in assessing a situation and simply admitting we don't know (Chaleff, 2009).

Overall, the Companions are quite honest in letting The Doctor know they don't have any solutions or information that can help the situation. They might offer something a bit off the cuff, but immediately admit they don't really know. Interestingly, Donna Noble is quite open about her skills as a temporary administrative assistant. In fact, her office skills are critical in understanding the use of clones at the ATMOS factory in *The Sontaran Stratagem* (2008) because she goes to the Human Resources Department to discover none of the employees have ever taken a sick day. This scene demonstrates how even those with a low status on an organizational chart can emerge as a leader due to their expert knowledge of how the system functions. In *Journey's End* (2008), she boasts of her typing skills as she hacks into the Dalek computer system at a rate boosted by her newfound Time Lord powers inadvertently gained by touching the Tenth's Doctor's regenerating hand. Additionally, she explains in excruciatingly detailed scientific language how she was able to achieve the defeat of the Daleks, which is in sharp contrast to how others have always seen her as flighty and not well-informed. But her knowledge is not to last. The Doctor must wipe her memories, or she will burn with the awareness of the Time Lords inside her human brain.

CONSCIENTIOUS ACCESS

Serving with courage goes beyond trust and communication to being conscientious about how much interaction you have with the leader. The Companions often wish they had more access to The Doctor than they receive. Amy Pond and Rory Williams flip-flop between needing a rest at home and the doldrums of housekeeping with their excitement and desire to go on another adventure (*The Power of Three*, 2012). They complain that it's been nearly nine months since they have heard from The Doctor and wonder if he has simply left them behind. This episode also includes the Eleventh Doctor staying with them for a few days, which seems to ensure they need to be careful what they wish for. Just as with the Companions, followers must be careful about the demands they place on a leader's time and maintain a balance that prevents undue pressure (Chaleff, 2009). Being conscientious about when – or if – attention is necessary from the leader is another opportunity for serving with courage.

The courageous follower doesn't need excessive access to a leader, as they have empowered themselves to make decisions and take the initiative. If they are sticking to the key guidelines of communication by bringing important issues to the leader with concise well-organized thoughts, they may very well feel as if their relationship is more distant than they would prefer. It's important to understand that conscientious access additionally requires maintenance of the leader–follower relationship. When we require access, those exchanges should be valuable and characterized by conversations that serve to recharge energies, stimulate the mind, demonstrate empathy, and even provide candor about difficult subjects, if necessary. Moreover, by conscientiously accessing contact with leaders we develop our ability to speak and act in the leader's name because we are staying tuned into the leader's values, priorities, and vision (Chaleff, 2009).

Martha Jones demonstrates the balance between needing access to The Doctor and being conscientious about that access. After Martha chooses to no longer travel with the Tenth Doctor as his Companion (*The Last of the Time Lords*, 2007), we discover she has become a highly placed member of UNIT, the Unified Intelligence Task Force that investigates extraterrestrial threats. When UNIT discovers that green technology installed in almost all vehicles may be of alien design, Martha contacts The Doctor through the cellphone, she left him for that purpose (*The Sontaran Stratagem*, 2008; *The Poison Sky*, 2008). Just as the Tenth Doctor and Donna Noble appear, Martha gives the order for a raid on the ATMOS factory that manufactures the alien devices. Martha clearly seeks The Doctor for assistance only he can provide and isn't troubling him with trivial things or general strategies about investigating the alien technology. She maintains a professional attitude, and her entire demeanor demonstrates her own empowerment and authority as she continues the mission to defend Earth. Martha reconnects with The Doctor and performs maintenance on their relationship, and she is also introduced to Donna, which gives her the chance to build an empathetic relationship with another Companion and mention some humorous unpleasant truths The Doctor is rather embarrassed about.

DEFENDING THE LEADER

As leaders are typically the most visible members of an organization, they are prone to be the object of complaints and receive the full blame for things that go wrong (Chaleff, 2009). Serving with courage calls on followers to defend the leader against these attacks. Of course, no leader is without flaws or accountability for poor decisions and lack of action. But just as followers should not follow blindly, they should not defend their leader blindly either as that action doesn't serve the leader, followers, or organization. Followers should differentiate the issues and be supportive in appropriate ways, but never cover up for a leader's imperfect conduct (Chaleff, 2009).

When there are internal complaints, courageous followers serve their leader by addressing the mood or attitudes that are fostering the complaints. Moods can be contagious and "there is a tendency for connected individuals to become more emotionally similar over time" (Block & Burnett Heyes, 2022, p. 1194). A negative mood can destroy the morale of a group or organization and be manifested through several behaviors, such as absenteeism or low productivity as well as steady complaining. It's very possible the complaints are legitimate, but the organization is not served when there is lack of mutual respect or attention to reaching shared goals because of dissatisfaction. Courageous followers remind those who complain about the leader's strengths and vision, which could be taken for granted by those complaining (Chaleff, 2009). In addition, followers who consider themselves to be serving the leader, but find themselves complaining can also reflect on their role and the courageous actions they can take to be more effective (Chaleff, 2009).

For Yasmin Kahn, Graham O'Brien, and Ryan Sinclair, their group begins to fracture when the Thirteenth Doctor is taken captive by the Judoon and imprisoned. She's been gone for 10 months. Yaz is obsessed with trying to find her and even sleeps in the abandoned TARDIS to continue her search among the information stored there. Graham and Ryan are concerned about Yaz's well-being and try to get her to understand The Doctor may not have survived whatever ordeal awaited her. Yaz doesn't want to hear that. Ryan complains it has been 10 months and they should get on with their lives. Yaz reminds Ryan, The Doctor saved them countless times. But then Graham shows her a video of a Dalek on Earth being used to police the United Kingdom and they determine to carry on the mission of taking care of things on planet Earth by discovering more about the Dalek (*Revolutions of the Daleks*, 2021). This scene with the Companions to the Thirteenth Doctor exemplifies how the absence of a leader can create low morale and lessen cohesion, but also how courageous companions can stifle those tendencies and use their dissatisfaction with the current situation to move forward and continue the overall mission and purpose.

There may be external instances when the leader's public image contrasts with their public behaviors. Courageous followers "prevent the leader's detractors from redefining [their] image based on behavior that was an exception" (Chaleff, 2009, p. 69). In *The Last of the Time Lords* (2007), the Tenth Doctor has been held captive by The Master and appears to be unable to overcome the Master's time trap and help the people of Earth against the tyranny of The Master and their impending destruction at the hands of the alien Toclafane. Martha Jones has been traveling the Earth as a wanted fugitive for the past year spreading hope among the people by telling the story of The Doctor and assuring them of The Doctor's faithfulness and trust-worthiness. His situation as a helpless prisoner is an exception to their notions of The Doctor.

Indeed, Martha's defense of The Doctor strengthens her emotional intelligence for social skill, in that she must create a vast network of humans around the globe who will work together to psychically overcome the technology of The Master and free The Doctor from his imprisonment. Conversely, Martha's courage in traveling around the Earth, developing a ruse by which to be taken back to The Master, and maintaining the secret The Doctor whispered to her before she left him, cultivates the way in which The Master, the greatest detractor of The Doctor, views The Doctor. The Master does not see The Doctor's acquiescence as atypical, but a result of The Master's superiority. Martha courageously allows this impression to continue, at the risk of her own life, until the moment she and The Doctor are ready to reveal their plan and defeat The Master (*The Last of the Time Lords*, 2007).

TENDING TO PHYSICAL AND EMOTIONAL NEEDS

Leadership exacts a toll on the body and the mental health of leaders. Not only can there be a sense of isolation from others due to the formal structure of an organization or lack of relationships with peers, but it can also be compounded by the mental pressures of being a leader and the responsibilities of creating a vision for the future and influencing others to reach those shared goals. Isolation and mental fatigue can lead to unhealthy behaviors that harm the body, whether it is overindulgence or not sleeping. Of course, there can be other instances when a leader is injured or becomes ill and is unable to meet their responsibilities, which also requires courageous followers to serve (Chaleff, 2009).

For example, in *The Christmas Invasion* (2005) and *Deep Breath* (2014) the Tenth and Twelfth Doctors, respectively, are recovering from their regeneration and unable to thwart the antagonists in the episodes from causing harm to Earth. As courageous Companions, Rose, Clara, and Madame Vastra must overcome their fears and grief for the loss of the previous incarnation of The Doctor and tend to the physical needs of the regenerating Doctor. Each knows they are "responsible for the welfare of the leader as a human being who is ill, and perhaps in pain and frightened" (Chaleff, 2009, p. 78). Rose makes certain the Tenth Doctor is given a place to sleep and watched over even as alien Santa Claus' wreak havoc across London (*The Christmas Invasion*, 2005). Madame Vastra understands that as the Twelfth Doctor is not able to meet his duties, she must take on the responsibilities and authority for learning how a dinosaur reached Victorian-era London, why it exploded, and who is responsible for the recent string of internal combustions (*Deep Breath*, 2014). More to the point, the Eleventh Doctor phones Clara in the future as he is on the verge of dying/regenerating and tells her that no matter how scared she might be about his new regeneration, the Twelfth Doctor is more scared than anything she can imagine, and he needs her help (*Deep Breath*, 2014).

Beyond the circumstances of when The Doctor is ill due to regeneration, Companions must be attuned to their emotional and mental health, which is quite difficult considering The Doctor suffers from guilt, regret, and shame for their actions during the Time War with the Daleks and the destructive behaviors they display throughout their journey. Companions often ask if The Doctor is okay, though they invariably respond they are fine and move the conversation to something else. For example, Donna Noble asks how the Tenth Doctor is doing after the death of River Song and he responds he is alright, to which Donna replies "Special Time Lord Code for really not alright?" (*Forest of the Dead*, 2008).

Yet, outside of the reluctance to discuss mental health there is also a sense of The Doctor having an addiction. Clara mentions this in *Mummy on the Orient Express* (2014) as they are taking a "last hurrah" trip because she has decided to stop traveling with The Doctor after her gut-wrenching experience making a choice about the survival of humanity (see *Kill the Moon*, 2014). She asks the Twelfth Doctor if he enjoys being the one to make impossible decisions because that is what he does all day, every day. She suspects he may have an addiction to taking risks, holding power, and being the one responsible for nearly everything. But then, Clara decides to continue traveling with The Doctor and lies about Danny Pink's approval of her decision. It would seem she is just as addicted to the excitement of traveling with The Doctor and living on the edge.

SUMMARY

Serving with courage requires followers to unburden the leader and make decisions or solve problems which serve the leader and organizational goals. It requires building and maintaining mutual trust, as well as a willingness to communicate and have difficult conversations when necessary. Serving with courage means followers need to be conscientious about their need for access to the leader and use the time in constructive meaningful ways. Followers must also defend their leader against internal dissention, such as complaints, and external opposition through reminding others of the leader's strengths and rationale for actions that may seem contradictory to their public personae without becoming a dishonest apologist. Finally, courageous followers serve the leader by being attuned to their physical and emotional well-being and temporarily assuming the duties of the leader to further the progress of the organization when they are unwell.

REFLECTIVE ACTIVITIES

- Consider a time when you felt the need to have a difficult conversation with your leader. If you didn't follow through, reflect on ways you might develop your courage to do so in the future and the action steps you will take to enable a positive, supportive difficult conversation. If you did follow through, reflect on the positive or negative outcomes of the conversation. What might you do differently in the future based on the concept of serving with courage? How will matters of mutual trust and a strong interpersonal relationship factor into your thinking?

- Many of us work in environments that cultivate a culture of complaining. Do you experience this in your workplace or other organization where you are a member, such as school, church, or community group? What steps might you take to demonstrate serving with courage to overcome the internal conflicts and defend the leader in a manner that is not confrontational or untruthful?

4

CHALLENGING THE DOCTOR WITH COURAGE

Rule number one: The Doctor lies.

What's a Companion to do when faced with following someone who can't always be trusted to tell the truth? If we consider the leader–follower relationship as crucial to the process of co-creating the leadership process and founded on trust, mutual values, shared goals, and candid communication, we need to be certain we can give constructive feedback to our leaders – even if that means calling them out on their lies. As Chaleff (2009) writes, leaders and followers "enter a type of sacred contract to pursue their common purpose" (p. 86) and followers are charged with holding the leader to the contract. This means Companions must challenge The Doctor when they lie, when they refuse to take help, and when they lose sight of shared purpose and values.

COMBATTING LEADER SELF-DECEPTION

There are numerous examples in our organizations and societies where an admired charismatic leader is ultimately discovered to be unethical, immoral, incompetent, or otherwise unfit to be in their position of authority. We will rightfully blame the leader for the problems that occur because of their behaviors or policies, but we rarely look at their followers as partners in the disastrous outcomes. Courageous followers must be willing to challenge their leader, either directly or indirectly, to preserve the organization and sustain the progress toward completing organizational goals.

Leaders can be characterized by strong egos and passionate visions, which can also lead to self-deception (Chaleff, 2009). These are the leaders who refuse to accept information that is counter to their thinking or stands in the way of achieving their vision. It is not uncommon for leaders mired in self-deception to be considered by others as charismatic leaders, but we need to remember the original understanding of charismatic leaders from Max Weber in the 1920s for defining charismatic leaders as divinely inspired with exceptional powers or qualities (Barnes, 1978) to realize these leaders can be dangerous and charisma "generates the risk of spawning monsters" (Pombeni, 2008, p. 37).

Is The Doctor a monster? Sometimes. Their arrogance and self-deception for considering themselves to possess God-like superiority and "failing to perceive their commonality" (Chaleff, 2009, p. 102) can lead to monstrous actions. Of course, it begins with the War Doctor believing he has the power and privilege to stop the Time War by destroying his entire planet and people of Gallifrey, and then killing millions of Daleks, as well. The Ninth Doctor uses a woman to open a rift and create an energy portal to remove an alien race, the Gelth, who were decimated by the Time War. The Doctor knows she will die. Rose Tyler accuses him of using her to fight his battles. The Ninth Doctor retorts, "It's a different morality. Get used to it or go home" (*The Unquiet Dead*, 2005). At the end of *The Family Blood* (2007), the Tenth Doctor places the Family into perpetual tortures with the father in chains, the mother in a prison at the edge of an event horizon, the son perpetually guarding the fields of England as a scarecrow, and the daughter imprisoned in every mirror for eternity. The son remarks they had experienced "the fury of a Time Lord" and when The Doctor ran away from them it was an act of kindness (*The Family Blood*, 2007). In *The Runaway Bride* (2006), the Tenth Doctor becomes consumed with rage he cannot control as he destroys the children of the Empress Racnoss. She is allowed to escape only due to the intervention of Donna Noble who tells him to stop.

These are the instances when it is imperative for the Companions to stand up to The Doctor. They must pull away the blinders of self-deception and reveal reality (Chaleff, 2009). In the aftermath of tragic behaviors or ruinous outcomes, the opportunity exists for followers to be courageous and challenge leaders to change their ways.

PROVIDING FEEDBACK

There's no sense in challenging leaders and trying to give them feedback if they aren't ready to listen to what is being said. Courageous followers must find the proper time and method for feedback to prevent the leader from being dismissive or defensive (Chaleff, 2009). This does take courage. It isn't easy to share with someone we are close to that they are adversely affecting the group or organization. We must overcome our own feelings of possibly being rejected and demoted to the out-group. But if we are focused on shared values and common goals, and if we want to support the leader, we will overcome our fears and act courageously.

As with any feedback we would give to anyone else, we want to be careful about accusatory tones or lack of specificity. Change won't occur if the feedback doesn't explicitly address the behavior or issue. A best practice is to call out the specific behavior, explain the harmful consequences and the potential harm if the behavior continues (Chaleff, 2009). When the inter-personal relationship is strong, followers can use "I" statements, which can help in deflecting blame, not sounding accusatory, and doesn't create a space for defensiveness. "I am concerned about what happened the other day" is very different from "You did a bad thing and nearly got us killed when you blew up that alien ship." We need to also be aware of how the language our leaders use can be harmful, either as an outright lie or a way of sanitizing actions and abusive behaviors and hold them up as an opportunity for leaders to engage in self-examination (Chaleff, 2009).

Sounds simple, right? Of course, we know from our own experiences it's much more emotionally complex and requires sensitivity, good timing, and courage. Courageous followers must create a path for constructive feedback to the leader that shares input in a spirit of respect and care for the leader and engages their service of being willing to communicate and solve problems (Chaleff, 2009). The Companions do develop this ability, particularly as their relationship with The Doctor matures. But they do have different styles. Donna Noble is forthright and may sound hypercritical at first glance, but her respect and care for The Doctor can still be noticed. Rory Williams tries to remain calm and supportive but then takes issue with many of The Doctor's plans, particularly when they involve the safety of Amy Pond (see *The Pandorica Opens*, 2010; *A Good Man Goes to War*, 2011).

INDIRECT CHALLENGES

Leaders can feel threatened by direct challenges or may feel overwhelmed and pressured by the crisis of the moment and determine they need to exert their authority and simply refuse input and feedback from their followers. In these circumstances, courageous followers need to find indirect methods to not only continue progress toward the goals but maintain the relationship, too (Chaleff, 2009).

The key is to find a way to reengage the leader into conversations where alternative solutions can be explored. This may involve asking simple questions, such as whether there is another way to look at the situation (Chaleff, 2009). This gives leaders a moment for reflection – a chance to breathe – and creates a space to see a different perspective. Clara Oswald accomplishes this in *The Day of the Doctor* (2013) when she asks the War Doctor, Tenth Doctor, and Eleventh Doctor what the promise of their name means and thereby gets them to reevaluate the destruction of Gallifrey. When Clara travels with the Twelfth Doctor, we see her skills as a teacher when she asks The Doctor probing questions which challenge his thinking. In fact, her ability to indirectly challenge The Doctor through questioning continues even after her death as The Doctor's memory of her is manifest in front of a chalkboard writing out questions to help him escape from his confession dial in *Heaven Sent* (2015).

Another way to indirectly challenge a leader is to ask how a third party might interpret their behaviors or policies. For The Doctor, this could be invoking an enemy or a lost loved one. Captain Jack Harkness usually fulfills this role in challenging whatever marginally ethical action or plan The Doctor could be scheming by straightforwardly asking what Rose Tyler or Donna Noble might think. Evoking Companions who are absent and for whom The Doctor grieves is not playing fair, but it is effective.

In a mature partnership, followers understand they have a duty to challenge poor decisions and confront bad behaviors without falling into the trap of being contentious and unsupportive. Once a courageous follower launches conversations in a nonconfrontational way that indirectly challenges a leader's actions or potential actions, options become available, and the leadership process is more fully activated.

It's important to understand that as courageous followers, we must also reflect upon our own actions and responsibilities and take ownership of our own failures and complicity in how the leadership is enacted within our group or organization. Challenging the leader is not a one-way street pointing only in the direction away from ourselves. We can't act from a position of casting blame onto others without thinking about how we could have acted sooner or differently to prevent or avoid problems. The Courageous Companions in *Doctor Who* may flirt with feelings of guilt or shame when they realize they could have done something differently, but they invariably use their self-awareness and ability to self-manage their emotions to move forward and find a solution or fix the problem.

SUMMARY

Courageous followers must be willing to challenge their leader, either directly or indirectly, to preserve the organization, achieve organizational goals, and maintain the mutual influence necessary for the leadership process to be effective. There is a need to call out detrimental behaviors or policies in an honest manner and stand up to the leader. Sensitivity to the ways in which feedback is given becomes paramount for ensuring the feedback is received and accepted. Followers must also reflect on their own behaviors that might be encouraging or reinforcing harmful behaviors from the leader.

REFLECTIVE ACTIVITIES

- Consider a leader you are familiar with – whether in your own life or one you have seen in the media – who displays harmful leadership characteristics such as arrogance, self-deception, physical or emotional abusive behaviors, and other unethical actions. What steps would you take to challenge this leader? What type of feedback does this leader need? Will you use direct or indirect methods? Refer to Chapter 1 and the previous discussion of emotional intelligence. How will your emotional intelligence skills come into play?

- Reflect on a time when you disagreed with a policy or had issues with the behavior of a leader. Create a short list of "I" statements that address the issue with specificity and clarifies what is needed. For example, "Research shows that this is not a successful strategy and I believe we should discuss alternatives." How might you be able to use these types of statements to diffuse future problems?

5

MEETING TRANSFORMATION WITH COURAGE

Challenging a leader with courage requires more than simply providing feedback and offering options for behaving differently or revising policy. There is always the possibility the leader will simply reject the advice and then we are left shrugging our shoulders and soothing ourselves with the stories of how we tried. That's not good enough to demonstrate our abilities as courageous followers. The process of leadership is undeniably a process of change. At its core is the understanding for influencing others to change in some way to meet a shared goal in the future. Maybe the change is to be more productive for increased sales goals, redesign jobs to accommodate remote work, or embrace diversity and inclusion throughout the organization. Whatever the shared goal may be, it demands a change in behaviors – not simply announcing a new policy. The leadership process exists in opposition to being stagnant and protecting the status quo. The leadership process is about transforming our circumstances to achieve the vision of a better future. Leaders and followers are vital in accomplishing that transformation through collaboration.

However, leaders can be hesitant to change their ways even if change benefits the organization. After all, they became leaders because of who they are (Chaleff, 2009). What the follower needs is the courage to serve the leader in ways that produce transformation. Followers must help leaders become fully changed persons more capable and effective in serving others and the goals of the organization, while not allowing defeatism or the constraints of the status quo to get in the way. Kegan and Lahey (2009) suggest that true leadership development requires "qualitative expansions of mind that significantly increase human capability at work... by renewing existing talent" (p. 6). Courageous followers work to renew themselves and their leaders in ways that increase their capabilities.

RESISTANCE TO CHANGE

To enact change, leaders and followers must overcome the resistance to change within themselves and the organization. People resist change for various reasons. For some, they simply have a blind resistance to change and an intolerance that is so embedded in their beliefs they reject change out of hand. Others may have a political resistance to change where they fear the loss of their status, compensation, role, or other organizational benefit. Still others will resist change on ideological grounds because they feel the change is mistimed or won't work, and their case is based on perceived intellectual differences with the proposed change (Yilmaz & Kiliçoğlu, 2013).

In essence, resistance to change centers on the fear of losing something. We can be anxious about whether we will lose our jobs outright or lose our sense of competence from the role we have if our job duties change. We can fear losing our relationships with others in the organization due to restructuring and the power base we hold within those relationships. This is true for peer relationships, but also the power we enjoy from our relationship with our leader or being the leader. We can fear the loss of comfort we have with the habits of the status quo, which gives us a sense of competence and psychological safety. Our initial reaction to change could be resistance because we have a cynical belief about change due to previous organizational failures in planned change, but the underlying cause of our resistance is commonly a simple fear of the unknown.

FOLLOWERS AS AGENTS OF CHANGE

Change agents are those individuals who have the capacity or find the opportunities to create transformation within their organizations by leveraging their relationships and influencing others as to the attractiveness and achievability of change (Brown et al., 2021). If we are to grow as followers and cocreate the leadership process, we need to develop the ability to act as agents of change and meet the transformations that happen around us with courage. Being a change agent certainly involves developing our own abilities and growing as an individual, but it also involves challenging the leader and providing feedback, as discussed in the previous chapter, bringing forward the change vision from the leader to others in the organization, and helping the leader to change in ways that make the accomplishment of goals easier.

Chaleff (2009) identifies followers as catalysts for leader transformation who play pivotal roles in the process through courageously expressing their opposition to problematic behaviors, acknowledging leader frustrations, and then reflecting similar leader behaviors back to them, refusal to justify destructive behaviors, and preventing leaders from blurring the line between self-identity and organizational purpose. This can be uncomfortable for the follower and the leader and can lead to confrontation and relational tensions. However, "for transformation to occur, relationship rules need to change" (Chaleff, 2009, p. 130), and we must use our emotional intelligence skills to provide an open space in which to take risks. The critical concept for meeting transformation with courage is to engage the leader in ways that raise their consciousness and expand their mind so they can renew themselves and their capabilities.

Courageous followers can accomplish this through identifying trans-formation resources, such as coaching, counseling, or team simulations. Ultimately, there must be a supportive environment where the leader knows they are not alone and there is a community standing by them as they take on the difficult transformations. Followers can also model behaviors they want the leader to emulate and imbue the process with empathy and compassion to contend with potentially ingrained misconceptions of caring for others as a weakness and postures of hubris (Chaleff, 2009).

Within the transformation process, followers need to be aware of their feelings and attitudes and not have unrealistic expectations about what the leader can and cannot change – and how fast that change might occur. Persistence is crucial, and the level of commitment to the leader–follower relationship and dedication to organizational goals must be strong enough to endure a long-term difficult process (Chaleff, 2009).

When the Twelfth Doctor introduces Clara Oswald to the crew of the spaceship *Aristotle*, he is still groggy from his recent regeneration and can't always think clearly, but tries to explain, "This is Clara, not my assistant, she's, uh... some other word." Clara helps by telling the crew she is his carer. The Doctor agrees. "She cares so I don't have to" (*Into the Dalek*, 2014). Clara is good natured about this because she has grown to understand the necessity of her ability to model empathetic behaviors and not be too impatient or unrealistic about The Doctor's capabilities. As a change agent, Clara's main concern is for The Doctor and holding the courage to help him become who he is capable of being and not the monster he has always thought.

There can be fears and resistance due to the ambiguity of a change in leadership, which typically foreshadows a change in organizational strategy and structure. Even if followers instigate the transformative change in a leader, there may be unintended consequences for which they are not prepared, such as the leader seeking other opportunities outside the organization or the weakening of their relationship and collaborative abilities within the leadership process. Nevertheless, those consequences must be met with courage and improved upon, if possible, through further actions and persistence.

COPING WITH THE TRANSFORMATION OF A LEADER

In leadership studies, the discussion of coping with transformation of a leader typically centers on when the leaders of an organization are replaced, which can be a difficult situation for followers. Because of the relationship built over time with the previous leader, followers can feel deep loss when that leader is promoted, transferred, or leaves an organization. But what happens when the leader transforms and stays in their role? A singular element that is fascinating about our discussion of followership and *Doctor Who* is the opportunity to explore how followers cope with the transformation of a leader literally transformed from one body to another, but still carrying the core of the leader they knew previously.

With any change comes a sense of loss, and it's important to understand how we cope with change. In 1969, Elisabeth Kübler-Ross published her seminal work *On Death and Dying* and offered a model of coping with loss known as the "5 Stages of Grief." In its current form, the model is known as the Kübler-Ross Change Curve® and provides insights into how we emotionally manage significant change or loss (Elisabeth Kübler-Ross [EKR] Foundation, 2023).

The First Stage we experience is Shock or surprise over the event itself. For the Companions, the surprise of The Doctor transforming in front of them with vast amounts of energy streaming from their eyes, mouth, and limbs is indeed quite shocking. Several Companions are privy to how The Doctor changes, including Rose Tyler witnessing the regeneration of the Ninth Doctor (*The Parting of the Ways*, 2005) and Rose, Donna Noble, and Jack Harkness during the regeneration of the Tenth Doctor, which continues his current form due to using energy from his severed hand which simply heals him without full regeneration. The Companion who most fully experiences the Change Curve is Clara Oswald in *The Time of the Doctor* (2013) as the Eleventh Doctor regenerates and the Twelfth Doctor appears in his stead. Although she knows this is inevitable and why, she is still unprepared and quite shocked at what is happening.

Followed closely to the initial shock is the Second Stage of Denial when there is disbelief and searching for any proof that what just happened isn't true. In *Deep Breath* (2014), we meet the Twelfth Doctor and Clara in Victorian-era London. Madame Vastra, a homo-reptilis once saved by The Doctor, Jenny, her human wife, and Strax, a Sontaran soldier consigned to live on Earth, are there because of the spectacle of the dinosaur in the Thames. Madame Vastra realizes The Doctor has just regenerated and will need assistance. Clara is very upset with the transformation and anxiously asks how they can change him back. Her remarks bother Madame Vastra, and she determines to interrogate Clara and her intentions. Clara tells her what happened after the regeneration on Trenzalore and states "The Doctor was gone." But Jenny explains that The Doctor is not gone and is upstairs in bed. Clara becomes annoyed and admits, "Okay, he changed."

The Third Stage is one of Frustration as there is dawning recognition that things will be different. This may cause anger as the comfortable habits of the status quo and previous relationship are lost. Clara quickly becomes frustrated and angry as she talks to Madame Vastra and Jenny. Madame Vastra pushes back on Clara's notion that The Doctor changed by saying, "He regenerated. Renewed himself." But Clara is having none of it as she says he doesn't look renewed, he looks older. She also angrily accuses Madame Vastra of judging her. But Madame Vastra turns that back on her by saying

"The Doctor regenerated in front of you. The veil lifted. He trusted you. Are you judging him?" Clara angrily scoffs at being called out on her biases and assumptions about age and physical appearance (*Deep Breath*, 2014).

From the emotional high point of shock through denial and frustration, morale hits the lowest point with the Fourth Stage of Depression. It's clear the previous relationship will never return, and this can lower moods and result in lack of energy or desire to engage. For Clara, this begins with Madame Vastra's comments that "The Doctor needs us. You more than ever. He is lost in the ruin of himself, and we must bring him home." But Clara doesn't engage with The Doctor immediately and work to reclaim her relationship with him. She determines to put her energies toward finding who is killing people by causing internal combustion (*Deep Breath*, 2014).

Depression marks the central point of the coping process, but it should not be inferred that each stage is completed in comparable amounts of time or that one does not move back and forth between stages (EKR Foundation, 2023). After all, things in the Whoniverse can be a bit wibbly-wobbly timey-wimey.

The Fifth Stage is one of Experimentation where tentative steps are taken to engage with the new situation. Clara sees an ad in a newspaper for "The Impossible Girl," which is one of the nicknames given to her by the Eleventh Doctor. She is convinced this is a message from the Twelfth Doctor, and perhaps his memory of her is returning. She meets him in a restaurant, and their interaction is one of experimentation as they both are tentative and unsure how to interact and connect with each other. Clara even tells him not to smile as she is very cross with him. As they attempt to free themselves from being held by a robot who wants their body parts, The Doctor abandons Clara as they are about to be caught. The next moments are quite important for Clara as she finds her courage in the face of death at the hands of the robot to trust The Doctor and knows that he will always have her back. And he does. However, this moment is undercut by Clara moving backward in the Change Curve a few days later and telling Madame Vastra she isn't sure who the Doctor is anymore (*Deep Breath*, 2014).

The next two stages are critical in making it through the process. The Sixth Stage of Decision is when there is a conscious willingness to learn how to work within the new situation, and feelings become more positive. And the final Seventh Stage is one of Integration where changes are incorporated and there is a sense of renewal. It's important to note that the Twelfth Doctor presents Clara with a new reality from which she must make her decision. He tells her he has made many mistakes and wants to do something about them. He tells her, quite bluntly, that he is not her boyfriend. When Clara protests that she didn't think he was, he explains that he didn't say it was her mistake. This puts their relationship on a different level for The Doctor. Clara still shares that she is sorry but doesn't know who he is anymore. At this point, the phone rings. As mentioned earlier, Clara receives a phone call from the Eleventh Doctor asking her to help the Twelfth Doctor and not to be afraid. The Twelfth Doctor accuses her of not seeing him, which will become an important aspect of his journey. Fortunately, Clara does make the decision to work within the new paradigm, and they go for coffee (*Deep Breath*, 2014). As their adventures continue, the Seventh Stage of Integration progresses, and they can reform their relationship, validate each other, and continue to co-construct the leadership process in service to their mission. An argument could be made that their relationship becomes stronger and more intimate by removing the distractions and adolescent misunderstandings of romantic feelings.

Importantly, when transformation occurs, either through behaviors followers exact as change agents or a full transformative regeneration, validation is needed to reinforce the changes and strengthen the relational bonds between followers and leaders (Chaleff, 2009). This requires followers to meet the transformation with courage and for leaders to have the courage to accept transformation as well.

SUMMARY

The leadership process is about transforming our circumstances to achieve the vision of a better future, and followers are charged with assuming responsibility to assist leaders in their transformative process. To enact change, leaders and followers must overcome the resistance to change within themselves and the organization. Followers are the catalyst for change and engage the leader in ways that raise their consciousness and expand their mind so they can renew themselves and their capabilities. Persistence is crucial, and the level of commitment to the leader–follower relationship and dedication to organizational goals must be strong. Followers must also be open to traveling through the grief process as they cope with transformative change which often incurs loss.

REFLECTIVE ACTIVITIES

- How resistant to change are you? Reflect upon your actions and beliefs as they connect to the level of change you are willing to accept on any given day. How might you alter your behaviors, attitudes, or beliefs to be more willing to accept change? Students may want to complete this online questionnaire to discover their resistance to change and how they compare to others. https://pluto.huji.ac.il/~oreg/questionnaire.php

- What are your abilities as a change agent? Review this chapter for the various characteristics of how followers act as change agents. Then, consider an organizational change you previously experienced – or one that may be happening now – that you favor and want to be implemented. How might you use your influence and develop your courageous abilities as a change agent to achieve the transformation?

- How do you cope with change? Consider a time of organizational change or loss you experienced. Map your emotional reactions to the change using the Kübler-Ross Change Curve®. What personal strengths did you discover? What stages will you need to attend to more patiently or fully when you must go through this process in the future?

6

PARTING WITH COURAGE

When our leaders make mistakes, act unethically or immorally, or behave in any ways that are counter to the values and norms of the organization or society, it takes courage to stand up to them, persuade them to see their errors, and help them change their behaviors and get back on the proper path. But sometimes, there are boundaries that are crossed in such an egregious manner that, as followers, we are left to question our own moral integrity and personal agenda. What kind of courage does it take to refuse to act? To blow the whistle? To break our relationship with the leader and withdraw support? To leave the organization? What kind of courage does it take to stay and work toward bringing the leader and organization back into line with fundamental values and basic decency?

The final dimension Chaleff (2009) discusses for his framework in courageous followership is the courage to take moral action, where "the follower is faced with the choice of whether to go along with the prevailing culture or to take a stand that may generate unpleasant and difficult personal consequences" (p. 148). There is no one correct way in which to take moral action. It depends on the individual and their perspective of the situation. What is important is to make a conscious decision that is in alignment with our personal values while maintaining our dedication to the overall mission and purpose of the organization. If we do not act with intentionality in our role as a courageous follower, we run the risk of "becoming automatons with a dulled sense of responsibility for our actions" (Chaleff, 2009, pp. 150–151) and incapable of serving the organization, the leader, or ourselves.

DUTY TO DISOBEY

When it becomes impossible to enact change through the courageous followership behaviors discussed in the previous chapters, we are faced with two choices: accept the unavoidable loss and gracefully align ourselves with the decision or refuse to support the policy or plan if it is morally unacceptable (Chaleff, 2009). Principled actions of dissent are always contextual and can include a range of behaviors but must be publicly displayed for the disobedience to have any form or substance beyond our own internal dissatisfaction. Disobeying takes tremendous courage as there are typically pressures to conform from others in the group, as well as the leader. Courage is also needed by followers to sustain opposition to a morally objectionable plan of action. Disobedience is vital when the basic rights and safety of others are jeopardized (Chaleff, 2009).

This is the situation where the Companions are often most necessary to The Doctor and to the fundamental values of their purpose. Sometimes, disobedience is done with a light touch. Clara teases the Twelfth Doctor when he tries to tell her what to do by saying, "You're not my boss, you're one of my hobbies" (*Into the Dalek*, 2014). Often, the Companions disobey because The Doctor is choosing to run away or leave them behind, and they believe it is better to stay or go with them to fight.

One example is Rory Williams staying with Amy Pond who has been imprisoned in the Pandorica box meant to hold The Doctor. Rory was shifted from his own life and time to that of a Roman Centurion in the British Isles by the rift in time (see *Cold Blood*, 2010). The Eleventh Doctor and Amy meet him again, and together they fight against an array of enemies of The Doctor who want to put him into the Pandorica. The Doctor decides he and Rory should leave, but Rory refuses to obey him. He cannot leave Amy behind unguarded (*The Pandorica Opens*, 2010). He watches over the Pandorica for centuries, keeping himself generally anonymous, and becomes a legendary figure of fulfilling one's duty (*The Big Bang*, 2010). If Rory had not summoned the courage to disobey The Doctor and demonstrate fidelity to Amy, it was possible the Pandorica would have been lost to history along with his wife and darkness would have extinguished all life in the universe.

And yet, Clara is caught in a trap of wanting to disobey and not being able to do so because all life on Earth depends on her making a terrible decision. In *Kill the Moon* (2014), the moon has gained mass and thrown the Earth in chaos with extraordinary tidal disasters and other calamities stemming from the destruction of ocean side cities. A rag tag group of humans with a modicum of astronaut experience have landed on the moon in a mission to destroy it using nuclear missiles. With The Doctor's help, they discover the moon has something inside of it that is alive. They must still make the decision whether to continue on the mission to destroy the moon, which may create further chaos on Earth due to pieces of the moon falling to Earth or wait to see what happens with the thing inside of the moon and risk total destruction of the Earth.

Clara asks the Twelfth Doctor what they should do. He says he sometimes has gray areas where he doesn't know what the proper future should be. He refuses to suggest a plan of action and retreats to the TARDIS. This is a decision for humans to make since it is their planet and their moon. He says, "Some decisions are too important not to make on your own" (*Kill the Moon*, 2014). Clara is devastated by the choice she must make. She wants to disobey, but there is no way to get out of the situation. Clara and the human astronaut decide to let the people of Earth decide. They broadcast to Earth and ask humans to turn out their lights if they want the moon to be destroyed or leave them on if they want the being inside the moon to survive. Earth decides to destroy the moon. At the last second, Clara decides to stop the nuclear countdown. The Doctor takes them to Earth to watch as a beautiful bird is hatched from the moon and flies away, leaving another moon egg in its rightful place (*Kill the Moon*, 2014).

When The Doctor casually remarks he thinks she did the right thing, Clara's anger comes pouring out. She wants to know if he knew everything would be okay, but he sidesteps and says he knew she would make the best choice and blathers on. Clara screams at him to shut up. She tells him his actions were cheap, pathetic, and patronizing. The Twelfth Doctor is taken aback because he thought he was respecting her. Through tears, Clara explains, "I nearly didn't press that button. I nearly got it wrong!" She tells him to clear off and not come back. She is done with him (*Kill the Moon*, 2014). The ingrained reaction to do as she is told backfired for them in this instance. There was a duty to disobey and compel The Doctor to stay engaged in the leadership process, but Clara's trust in him evaporated her own agency. She would not repeat this.

WITHDRAWING SUPPORT

While whistleblowers are not always courageous followers, a courageous follower who must come to the decision of blowing the whistle on immoral or illegal activity has typically attempted other avenues of influence first. They realized any words of assurance that things are not as they seem or will change soon are false, and they pay attention to the actions of the leader. As the saying goes, watch what they do not what they say. Also, there can be a "crisis of identity" (Chaleff, 2009, p. 154) when followers have lost the essence of who they were prior to their relationship with the leader or organization, or they identify so fully with the leader and shared purpose it can be frightening to think about leaving.

The Viking girl, Ashildr, is one of the few characters who withdraws support from The Doctor. After becoming immortal through alien technology in *The Girl Who Died* (2015) and determining her identity will simply be "Me" after centuries of living, she decides to do what she can to thwart The Doctor. She understands they are dangerous and have little regard for others. They have too much power that can be abused. Me has had a crisis of identity from the pain of being immortal and blames The Doctor. His actions do not align with his words. If he cared about her, he would not have sentenced her to immortality (*The Woman Who Lived*, 2015; *Face the Raven*, 2015; *Hell Bent*, 2015).

LEAVING

When a follower parts ways with a leader or organization, it doesn't necessarily mean it is done because the follower is taking a moral stand against bad actions or cannot reconcile feelings of betrayal or fear. Sometimes, followers leave because they can't seem to find the key to building a solid relationship with the leader. Followers can also leave because of their own personal growth and need to seek out new opportunities or be of use in other places. Sometimes, our best efforts to be a change agent and bring new life to an organization or improve behaviors simply fail, and we need to move on (Chaleff, 2009).

The ability for leaders to mentor their followers is a strong characteristic within effective leadership activities. The development of interpersonal relationships and moving a follower through the phases of the leader–member exchange (LMX) theory – from stranger to acquaintance to mature partner – requires a certain level of mentoring. There is usually a positivity bias in thinking about mentor relationships as being free from conflict or relational difficulties, but these relationships are no different than any other human relationship and fall along an unfixed continuum (Johnson, 2003). However, what is often missed is the understanding that at some point the relationship will shift as the protégé outgrows their need for a mentor or develops their own perspective in contrast to that of the mentor. In a classical understanding of mentors, it is a necessity for the mentor to absent themselves so the protégé can reach their full potential (Campbell, 1949).

Regardless of the circumstances leading up to the decision to part ways, it takes courage to not only make that decision but to also follow through and leave. In *Doctor Who*, we find several examples of how the Companions part with courage.

Martha Jones leaves the Tenth Doctor after the terrible events of The Master and Traclafone (*Last of the Time Lords*, 2007). Her family was intimidated, tortured, enslaved, and nearly died because of their connection to her and her work on behalf of The Doctor. She tells The Doctor she can't leave the people of Earth, either. Martha then turns back to him and explains how she loves him, but he doesn't love her. It's too hurtful to continue traveling in that way. It took courage to admit that to The Doctor, but in so doing she was able to leave on her own terms and with a healthy attitude. She continues the mission of defending Earth as a member of the Unified Intelligence Taskforce (UNIT) and keeps in touch with The Doctor (*The Sontaran Stratagem*, 2008). She even mentions to Donna Noble she is "better for having been away" from The Doctor (*The Poison Sky*, 2008).

Mickey Smith leaves Earth and decides to remain in the parallel universe where his grandmother is still alive and he can join the Resistance fight against the Cybermen (*Rise of the Cybermen*, 2006). Although he was only a casual traveler with The Doctor and did it mostly to stay close to and protect Rose Tyler, his experiences affected him, and he has incorporated The Doctor's purpose of defending the Earth into his own personal mission. It takes courage to leave your planet, even if you are going to another Earth in a parallel universe. Mickey risks not only his life as a Resistance fighter, but he risks never seeing those he loved. Fortunately, Mickey does return to Earth and continues to defend the Earth (*The Stolen Earth*, 2008; *Journey's End*, 2008).

Dan Lewis says goodbye to traveling with The Thirteenth Doctor and Yasmin Khan after a relatively short time and never quite meets the full Mature Partner stage but is a close and valuable Companion, nonetheless. When the trio returns to Earth after an unsuccessful attempt to intervene against Cybermasters who attacked a bullet train in space, Dan tells The Doctor not to come back for him. His near-death experience has changed him. "I was one hand away from flying off into space and suffocating... All of this is amazing, and I've had an incredible time, but it's not my life" (*The Power of the Doctor*, 2022). Though his life on Earth before he met The Doctor was not very fulfilling, and his house is gone due to a trap set by Karvanista (see *The Halloween Apocalypse*, 2021), Dan tells The Doctor he can get back to his life, confront it, and do better because of his experiences with her (*The Power of the Doctor*, 2022). Even in his short journey with The Doctor, he defies his own expectations and grows into a man who has the courage to meet the challenges of his life and succeed.

Ryan Sinclair had a more difficult time mustering the courage to leave The Doctor. His dissatisfaction began when he checked in with a good friend to find he was not doing well, and it wasn't only because everyone was having nightmares (*Can You Hear Me?*, 2020). He promises to stay in touch with his friend but finds it difficult with all the traveling. Ryan confides in Yasmin Khan that he worries they are living at different rates than their family and friends, which puts a strain on their lives. The situation comes to a head in *Revolution of the Daleks* (2021), when the Thirteenth Doctor was missing for 10 months in a Judoon prison and Ryan tells Yaz and Graham it might be time for them to move on with their lives. Even when The Doctor returns, there is an awkwardness, and Ryan summons up the courage to call her out for glossing over real issues and pretending everything is fine. At the end of the episode, Ryan tells the group he is going to stay home. He believes his friends need him, and he feels the planet does, too. Graham O'Brien decides to stop traveling with The Doctor as well so he can spend more time with Ryan. After successfully and bravely fighting for other planets in *Ascension of the Cybermen* (2020), he appears to want to fight for his own planet now (*Revolution of the Daleks*, 2021).

The decision to leave The Doctor was not easily arrived at for Ryan. It took a while to simmer in his mind as he weighed the advantages and disadvantages. The choice did not seem to be one spark but a cumulative effect of exhaustion, fear, and regretting the loss of relationships he had before he met The Doctor. His personal growth developed through his adventures and through the time when The Doctor was absent and enables him to show the courage of his own convictions and make a way for himself that still includes defending Earth but being present for others in life, too. Ryan's example is not markedly different from that of many of us who eventually realize we must move on from our organizations and those we follow to courageously head off to make our own path.

STAYING

As Chaleff (2009) points out, "courage is not absolute" (p. 177), and we shouldn't judge the choices of others on this account. Even if we have a moral obligation to leave, there are times we can justify staying, such as rationalizing our presence to oppose organizational extremists, skepticism that any other opportunity exists, or we simply need our job to pay the bills. Perhaps we stay because we have seen organizational change before and believe we can simply wait it out and problems will be magically resolved (Chaleff, 2009).

Courage is needed when deciding to stay, but the necessary courage is to be brutally honest with oneself. There can be no self-deception that we aren't supporting unethical or immoral behaviors by our presence, that we "had no choice," or there is nothing we can do about any of it (Chaleff, 2009). Importantly, courageous followers must continue to function as agents of change even if those actions are very small and quiet. Those who stay and continue to inspire change are similar to the "tempered radicals" described by Debra Meyerson. These are people who want to remain part of their organizations even if they feel their values or identity does not entirely fit with the dominant culture. Tempered radicals "are quiet catalysts who push back on prevailing norms, create learning, and lay the groundwork for slow but ongoing organizational and social change" (Meyerson, 2003, p. 166).

The Osgoods are a great example of those who decide to stay within their organization and work to generate social justice from the inside. The Osgoods are identical life-forms with one being human and the other being a shape-shifting Zygon. As scientific advisors for UNIT, they are indispensable in keeping the peace between humans and the Zygons who are refugees on Earth that take human form to live their lives in peace (see Chapter 8 for a more thorough discussion of The Osgoods). But The Osgoods encounter microaggressions about their nature. People continually think one Osgood must be "real" and human, while the Zygon sister must be illegitimate. They are questioned, but they refuse to answer which is which. The Twelfth Doctor invites Osgood to travel with him and Clara on the TARDIS, but she declines because she and her sister have work to do defending Earth and, presumably, bringing greater understanding of diversity and inclusion to UNIT (*The Zygon Inversion*, 2015).

SUMMARY

No matter how strong our relationship to a leader or our dedication to an organizational purpose is, there can be situations of immoral, unethical, illegal actions that cause followers to take a moral stand and part with a leader or organization. Followers may feel a duty to disobey or withdraw their support of a leader. Leaving can be a difficult decision, but maintaining the courage to act in connection with personal values or to seek new opportunities due to outgrowing the organization is a key quality of a courageous follower. Even those who choose to stay must continue their courageous actions, even if limited in scope, to maintain their moral integrity.

REFLECTIVE ACTIVITIES

- Have you ever been faced with an order or organizational practice you found morally unacceptable? Perhaps you disagree with public policy or government practices. What was your response? Did you accept the situation, or did you refuse to obey? What actions did you take to accept or refuse? Did those actions align with your personal values and maintain your moral integrity? What might you do differently to act with courage in the face of unethical or immoral circumstances?

- Have you ever left or considered leaving an organization or group of which you were an engaged member due to seeking more personal fulfillment? Reflect on that experience and consider the courageous actions you took to leave. If you did not leave, but only considered doing so, how might your new understanding of courageous followership allow you to leave – or stay – with courage?

- How might you proactively prepare to meet moral challenges in the future with courage? Give yourself some time to reflect on your personal values, moral and ethical perspectives commitment to the shared purpose of the organization or group and to the leader. What might be situations you think would cross the boundaries of your acceptance. Develop a plan for how you will meet that challenge. Consider your tolerance for ambiguity and tolerance for risk as you think about your plan. Run through the various actions you will take and the justifications for those actions. Be honest with yourself. Whether you leave or stay, make sure you know why and how you will meet the challenge with grace and courage.

- Now that you have read about each of the five dimensions for being a courageous follower and examples of various Companions, think about which quadrant you might place the Companions discussed in the book. Chaleff (2009) describes his typology of followers as four quadrants: Resource, Individualist, Implementer, and Partner with differing levels of support and willingness to challenge the leader (refer back to Chapter 1 for a refresher on the typology). Which Companion belongs to which quadrant and what evidence supports your thinking? Is there a quadrant that is empty or overfilled? What might account for this?

7

THE OBLIGATIONS OF THE DOCTOR

The previous chapters have explored the five dimensions of followership and idealized leader–follower relationship as outlined by Chaleff (2009). We now turn our attention to the enriching behaviors that deepen the symbiotic relationship between leaders and followers in co-constructing the leadership process through challenging the hierarchy and having the courage to listen to followers. Just as the leader we follow in an organization may not be the ultimate person in charge, in *Doctor Who* we discover that The Doctor is not the highest authority in the universe either. And yet, to enact change through the leadership process, The Doctors and Companions are obliged to courageously speak up to and challenge the hierarchy. As leaders have an obligation to listen to their followers with courage and accept their support and input, this enriching behavior is crucial for The Doctors.

Humans are social animals, and we have developed social and organizational structures to contain order within our societies and organizations. When a hierarchical structure is created, there is always an indication of power – who has it and who doesn't. Those at the top possess legitimate power of authority by holding a formal role – whether they are a head of state, religious leader, or clan chief. In organizations, the CEO, Board of Directors, and others in top management hold the power and authority. The hierarchy is very invested in maintaining their power and the status quo. After all, their decisions created the status quo, and it benefits them and their closest followers. But a hierarchy can also be very insulated and removed from the daily issues and concerns faced by those in the lower rungs of society or an organization. Consequently, as Chaleff (2009) explains, it takes courage to challenge the hierarchy through reducing learned helplessness, properly communicating the facts and data in a way that captures their attention, educating them, and speaking up.

REDUCING LEARNED HELPLESSNESS

In large organizations, there are often so many people that any initiative can get mired in the decision-making process as proposals make their way up the chain of command. A follower without courage may throw up their hands and deny any responsibility for a proposal or the potential outcomes. They determine they are at the mercy or whims of those above them in the hierarchy and lack any control. A courageous follower assumes responsibility and accountability for a proposal even if it has been revised beyond recognition. This courageous follower is fighting against the concept of learned helplessness. They do not allow themselves to fall victim to the excuse of "too many hands" on a proposal or project and the urge to feign helplessness to enact needed change (Chaleff, 2009). These followers find new solutions and don't allow past experiences to dissuade them. "One pair of committed hands, at a critical time and place, can provide the balance that rights a hierarchy that is tipping in an ill-advised direction when incomplete, manipulated, or misinterpreted data threaten to generate poor or dangerous decisions" (Chaleff, 2009, p. 186).

In *The Day of the Doctor* (2013), a nuclear countdown has been started by Kate Stewart, the head of the Unified Intelligence Taskforce (UNIT), which will destroy all of London and the invading Zygon shape shifters. The Tenth Doctor, Eleventh Doctor, and War Doctor have come to the Black Archives of UNIT to try and stop that possibility. Even with the power of three Time Lords in the same space and time, a resolution is not guaranteed. The War Doctor is also preoccupied with his own challenge of whether to detonate the "Moment" weapon in his own time. To do so would bring about the end of the Time War with the Daleks, destroy the planet Gallifrey, but also save many lives in the long term. Clara Oswald has a quiet moment with the War Doctor where she mentions how he seems so young and not yet burdened with the awful knowledge of his future to come due to the action he is contemplating.

The Doctors do broker a peace that prevents nuclear holocaust between humans and Zygon. The Tenth Doctor and Eleventh Doctor return to Gallifrey and the War Doctor's time to help the War Doctor make his choice for the destruction of Gallifrey. They are determined to push the button together so that it isn't a burden for just the War Doctor. Clara stands by in tears as they are about to push the button. She is horrified to be witnessing The Doctors kill the men, women, and children of Gallifrey. In fact, the Tenth Doctor calculated he killed 2.47 billion children that day (*The Day of the Doctor*, 2013). Clara labels them the Warrior and the Hero but scoffs that any idiot can be a hero. She wants them to be a Doctor. She asks them about that name. She was told the name they chose was a promise, but what was it? They answer their promise was to never be cruel or cowardly; to never give up and never give in. They set an obligation for themselves, and they are on the verge of not living up to it.

Just then, the Eleventh Doctor has an inspiration, one that has taken 400 years to germinate, and they create a plan that does not involve destroying Gallifrey. They use their TARDISes to freeze Gallifrey into a pocket universe that will hold it in a single moment of time and give the people hope for survival. Their other regenerations arrive with their TARDISes to join them in the effort, and all thirteen Doctors successfully work together to meet the objective of saving the people and planet of Gallifrey (*The Day of the Doctor*, 2013).

In this example, there is the learned helplessness of The Doctor for thinking the past cannot be changed and their fate is to always be the one who is the Destroyer of Worlds and the scourge who obliterated their own planet and peoples. In the ensuing centuries, they have purposefully buried the memory of their actions and pretended the War Doctor never existed. But they have Clara Oswald as their courageous Companion who pushes aside their misconceptions and flawed mental models to reignite the consciousness for their obligation for why they do what they do. She challenges these Time Lords so they can, in their turn, challenge the hierarchy of the Gallifreyan Time Lord Council ineffectively fighting the Daleks and present their solution for ending the Time War. Her presence at this critical moment in their history and provoking renewed commitment to their mission and purpose serves as the balance to keep them from making a devastating decision. Her sense of agency flows to them, and they have the recharged ability to change history and save the Time Lords from extinction.

COMMUNICATING INFORMATION APPROPRIATELY

The Doctor is very good at seeking out facts and data to help them solve a mystery or correct a problem. They are also tremendously self-assured in their analysis of facts and data as to what actions should be taken. But they do not often remember to communicate that information in ways that effectively influence the hierarchy and grab their attention. The Doctor does not always understand they cannot demand action but must make an informed recommendation to those with greater authority. This requires a Companion to step in, make a request, and add the missing information that will influence the powerful to act in ways that prevent further disaster.

Of course, the opposite can be true and The Doctor rattles off too much information that becomes an incoherent word salad to others, and the Companion steps in to succinctly share the information. Other instances include The Doctor simply disregarding any issue of interest to the hierarchy in favor of their own analysis and focus and declaring that something won't work, whereas the Companion steps in to find a way of incorporating the analysis of the authority.

In *Listen* (2014), the Twelfth Doctor is painting a pessimistic picture of life to the young Rupert (Danny) Pink. The boy asks if he is safe after having a ghostly apparition in his bed. The Doctor tells him no one is safe in the dark and anything can get him. That he is all alone. Clara smacks The Doctor on the head to shut him up and stop him from scaring the child. The Doctor insists people shouldn't be lied to, but Clara continues by telling Rupert the plastic soldier toys he has will keep him safe. This is communication that is appropriate for a child and instills a sense of well-being. The story also helps The Doctor witness empathy in action and learn to listen for himself.

The scenarios point toward the importance of the co-constructed leadership process perspective and the critical obligation of developing a strong interpersonal relationship between leaders and followers. They cannot be successful and meet their purpose if they do not work together and complement each other in ways that allow them to not only be courageous in the situations where they have power and control but also when they must petition higher authorities for moral action. For leaders and followers to be successful in their appeals, they must communicate information in a compelling manner that captures the attention of the hierarchy by framing the issue in ways that hold their interest and be prepared to competently suggest actions to take and the likely outcomes (Chaleff, 2009).

SHARING INFORMATION AND SPEAKING TRUTH TO POWER

In contemporary organizations, knowledge is no longer owned by the top leaders but exists throughout the organization and often resides in the lower echelons or on the front line. The knowledge worker economy has created a more egalitarian base of institutional expertise through specialization, and the hierarchical structure creates functional silos where communication processes may be compromised. Even though the increase of the Millennial and Gen Z cohorts entering the workplace have demonstrated a generational gap of knowledge, particularly in terms of technology and digital communication commonly used in the workplace (Berger, 2023), younger employees have opportunities to share knowledge of emerging technologies and trends with more tenured employees. Chaleff (2009) advises leaders to be prepared to educate the hierarchy and points out, "new patterns of thinking and possibility... must be integrated into the mental maps of the organization's leaders" (p. 191). Followers need to expect they will be asked to educate their supervisors and those farther up the hierarchy on their expertise and help them create new strategies and policy in an ever-changing environment. Followers must be able to meet this challenge with courage through being confident, clear, patient, and assuming responsibility for the information and guidance being shared (Chaleff, 2009).

In *Doctor Who*, sharing information to the powerful and the education of the hierarchy often involves simply explaining human behaviors and advocating for planet Earth to not be destroyed by alien life-forms. Rose Tyler takes on this responsibility for the Tenth Doctor who is absent while regenerating. Rose takes control of the situation, cutting off Prime Minister Harriet Jones, and speaks directly to the Sycorax herself. She demands they release their hold on humans and leave Earth's atmosphere (*The Christmas Invasion*, 2005). She doesn't quite succeed in her bluff for quoting the intergalactic Shadow Proclamation laws, but the demonstration of courage to stand up to these aliens on their own spaceship is an important showcase for her confidence and ability to take on the obligations of The Doctor during his absence and further co-construct the leadership process by challenging the powerful.

In *The Last of the Time Lords* (2007), Martha Jones courageously stands before The Master and laughs at him as he threatens her with death. She tells The Master she has no weapons, just words. For over a year, she has been telling the story of The Doctor to everyone across the planet so they can all come together in hope to think of his name and cause The Master's satellite system to fail which will free The Doctor. Even knowing The Master could kill her or her family at any moment does not detract Martha from speaking the truth to The Master and demonstrating the great courage she shares with The Doctor in their leadership process.

Of course, The Doctor must also hear the truth. Rory Williams is worried about a plan they have devised that puts Amy Pond at risk in *The Vampires of Venice* (2010). Rory asks the Eleventh Doctor if he really knows what makes him dangerous, "It's not that you take risks. It's that you make people want to impress you. You make it so they don't want to let you down. You have no idea how dangerous you make it for people when you're around" (*The Vampires of Venice*, 2010). The Doctor hears him but is not yet ready to accept what Rory has said.

Even Pete Tyler, from the parallel universe where Rose never became his daughter, tells the Tenth Doctor, "You're not in charge here and you're going to listen" and then proceeds to talk The Doctor and others into a plan for attacking the Cybermen (*Doomsday*, 2006).

The key to understanding the enriching behavior of challenging the hierarchy through reducing learned helplessness, communicating appropriately, and speaking truth to power is by examining the ways in which leaders and followers who are involved in the co-construction of the leadership process use their influence between each other and for sharing information and hard truths to those who have greater power than themselves. The leader has an obligation to understand their role in this process to create effective compelling proposals for action. As Chaleff (2009) notes, it takes persistence and a hopeful outlook to serve with courage against the obstacles while being patient for change to occur at the top.

ACCEPTING SUPPORT

Chaleff (2009) asks the question of whether leaders want courageous followers. Courageous followers can often bring bad news, dissenting opinions, complaints, and seek engagement on issues that are difficult to talk about. Although leaders may say they want their followers to come to them and have an "open door" policy, the reality is that many leaders would settle for an Implementer. It's just easier to have people who will simply implement the policy or action without challenging, though the risk of failure is higher when critical thinking and openness to alternatives is quashed (Chaleff, 2009). Even The Doctor will lose their temper with their Companions when the Companions want to argue a point or offer other solutions. In *The Vampires of Venice* (2010), the Eleventh Doctor angrily tells Amy Pond, "We don't discuss this, Amy. *I* tell you to do something and *you* do it!"

But when a leader understands their role in the leadership process as one of co-construction and interdependence with the follower, good things can happen. There is certainly less pressure upon the leader to be the sole problem-solver, but there is also an obligation placed on the leader to be open to the support and input from those around them. Leaders often work extensive hours and there may be a corporate culture that expects, if not rewards, long hours as a measure of toughness (Chaleff, 2009). It's important for leaders to understand they have an obligation to their self and to accept support from their followers to achieve goals.

The Doctor has a reputation for wanting to be in control and not allow others to take on their burden. This is combined with an inability to be still, though the Twelfth Doctor does try meditating on the top of the TARDIS (*Listen*, 2014), and it becomes clear The Doctor can become overworked and exhaustion could cause mistakes to be made. And when one is on an adventure with The Doctor, a mistake could mean the difference between life and death for everyone in a galaxy. The Companions discover the importance of building trust with The Doctor so they can be of service to them and the mission.

Beyond the knowledge of The Doctor as needing to be in control, what every Companion seems to know is the Doctor cannot travel alone. Particularly as they are saying their goodbyes, they remind The Doctor not to be alone. The rule goes beyond a simple need to not be lonely. The Companions provide the support The Doctor needs to stay focused, act with moral integrity, rein in destructive excesses, and have an audience for ideas and plans. The Doctor understands this about their own character, too, and accepts the obligation and support Companions offer so they do not travel alone.

APPRECIATING INPUT

Even when leaders accept support, they may not always appreciate the input they receive. Courageous followers can challenge a leader's style or strategy, which can cause defensiveness. Chaleff (2009) states it is critical for good leaders "to override naturally defensive feelings, statements, and behaviors, and display genuine interest in what sources of critical feedback are telling you" (p. 217). Creating a culture of open communication and showing appreciation, not defensiveness, for feedback is an obligation leaders owe their followers and organizations.

While The Doctor seldom waits for the input of others, they do have an appreciation for what they receive and rarely denigrate what is offered. The Doctor doesn't limit feedback to Companions and other followers. Unsurprisingly, they also appreciate input from themselves. When the Thirteenth Doctor is trapped and lost in the matrix on Gallifrey, she begins to question her entire existence after The Master shared her past as the original regenerating being who came to Gallifrey as a child. The Fugitive Doctor appears to her and listens as she expresses her doubts and what she might be able to do now that she knows the truth. The Fugitive Doctor scoffs and asks her, "Have you ever been limited by who you were before?" The Thirteenth Doctor pauses and notes that sounds like something she would say (*The Power of the Doctor*, 2022).

SUMMARY

In this chapter, we looked at the obligation leaders have toward their followers to challenge the hierarchy, reduce learned helplessness, communicate, speak truth to power, accept support, and appreciate input. These enriching behaviors reinforce the five dimensions of courageous followership. Leaders must overcome their defensiveness and be genuinely open to what others offer.

REFLECTIVE ACTIVITIES

- Reflect on a time when you had to speak with confidence and expert knowledge to someone who held more power or authority than you. What emotions did you feel? Were you anxious or nervous? Were you excited for the opportunity? Afterward, how did you think about the experience? Did you decide not to do that again or did you consider looking for additional opportunities? How important is it for you to be able to educate and inform the hierarchy for your personal growth and career progression?

- Consider the spaces in your life where you are a leader. This could be at your workplace or when you work on team projects at school or in the community. Your leadership practice could even be in your home with your family or roommates. Do you tend to want to do everything yourself? Do you work long hours and rarely accept help from others or delegate tasks? How does this affect your effectiveness as a leader? Do you find yourself overly involved in some areas, while neglecting others? What obligation do you have to yourself and to others for creating an environment of care and collective responsibility? What steps might you take to accept support from others to lessen the burden you carry?

- Reflect on the behaviors of your current leader. Do they tend to be defensive when you or others try to offer support or give input on a decision or action plan? What steps might you take as a courageous follower to help them overcome their defensiveness and build a stronger interpersonal relationship that allows them to fulfill their obligations to you and the organization more effectively?

8

THE COURAGE TO LOVE, FORGIVE, AND SEEK REDEMPTION

As I was researching and reflecting on courageous followership and the Companions in *Doctor Who*, I discovered there are missing aspects in discussions of followership. I have previously written about the leadership principles of love, forgiveness, and redemption (Yost, 2014) and believe they are similarly useful concepts in a discussion of followership. In fact, I consider them to be important correlations to emotional intelligence and help us to develop those skills more fully.

It takes courage to overcome our fears to love, forgive, and seek redemption. These principles are important in our real-life interpersonal relationships and are useful in furthering our understanding of the courageous follower and their relationship to their leaders in co-constructing the leadership process. But what is meant when we talk about love, forgiveness, and redemption in the context of followers and leaders?

LOVE

While The Doctor falls in love romantically with several Companions, our discussion of love will center on acts that provide for the common welfare. Oord's (2010) definition, "to love is to act intentionally, in sympathetic response to others ... to promote overall well-being" (p. 15), provides the framework for our discussion. This definition highlights the concept of love as an action – not merely a feeling – that is concerned with well-being and the dyadic relational nature of nonromantic love. Oord (2010) explains, "we are essentially related to others...If what we do partly determines who others become, and others partly determine what we become, our attempts to promote well-being in others often will increase our own well-being" (p. 57). As we explore the co-construction of the leadership process and understand how followers and leaders complement each other and rely on each other to develop their capabilities, the idea that these actions come out of love becomes rather apparent. The Companions care about the well-being of The Doctor. Who they become as courageous Defenders of the Earth is determined by their relationship with The Doctor, and who The Doctor becomes is determined by the influential courage and care of the Companions.

However, when considering social justice, sometimes it is necessary to act in ways that are hurtful for a few (Oord, 2010). The philosopher Pierre Teilhard de Chardin wrote about a love–energy that can change "culture, social institutions, and human beings" (King, 2004, p. 77). This love-energy, which takes a step beyond empathy, creates unity and applies the concept of love to the overall well-being of societies and cultures, not just individuals, even though the efforts may cause pain and hardship on those who have been the instigators of oppression or some of those trying to be helped may be lost.

In *Planet of the Ood* (2008), we discover the Ood are being surgically engineered to create docile servants and sold across the galaxies. At first, Donna Noble is disgusted by their features, but upon hearing the song of the Ood lamenting their torture and slavery, her aversion turns to compassion, and she is fundamentally changed in her assessment of the Ood by the power of their song that is steeped in their culture and communication practices. She begs the Tenth Doctor to do something to bring justice to the Ood. While their success in liberating the oppressed Ood harms the corporate slavers and those who depend upon the labor of slaves, applying the concept of love to the Ood society and culture is a definitive moment in the relationship between Donna and The Doctor, and has important consequences for Donna's future as a revered legend in Ood history. Donna is not only able to influence The Doctor and others to bring justice to the Ood, but she also furthers The Doctor's empathetic development which began with their first adventure in *The Runaway Bride* (2006) when she was able to stop the Tenth Doctor as he was consumed by anger in his destruction of the Empress of Racnoss and her children. Indeed, as Donna Noble develops her own courage, emotional intelligence, and follower skills, she affects The Doctor in ways that increase his emotional and psychological well-being, which in turn, increases her own well-being. Their interdependence is critical in co-constructing the leadership process and comes from loving actions that promote well-being and social justice. That interdependence is highlighted by the Ood naming her Doctor Donna (*Planet of the Ood*, 2008).

FORGIVENESS

It's important to understand what it means to forgive. As Madsen et al. (2009) explain, "forgiveness is not condoning, forgetting, or ignoring a hurtful action" (p. 248). The person who has been hurt needs to rid themselves of resentment or feelings of revenge and allow the person who hurt them to make amends, which changes the relationship in positive ways and minimizes the negative effects (Madsen et al., 2009). Importantly, forgiveness is a process. The person who has been hurt must re-forgive the wrongdoer each time they interact by being self-aware of the possible trigger to their emotions and managing those emotions. Sometimes that is done consciously, but over time, forgiveness becomes an unconscious behavior. This may be why we think of it as forgetting or ignoring.

Still, many of us have experienced being forgiven for a transgression and then much later having our wrongdoing brought back up to us and needing to make amends once again. Amy Pond repeatedly mentions the fact that the Eleventh Doctor left her waiting years for his return when she was a child, and The Doctor repeatedly apologizes. Amy must reassess her relationship with The Doctor each time she feels she is being abandoned or neglected and each time she must make a conscious decision to forgive and engage in the relationship once again. Amy's feelings of abandonment are reignited in *The Girl Who Waited* (2011) as she must wait 36 years on the planet Apalapucia for The Doctor and Rory to rescue her from a timestream that moves faster than theirs. The Older Amy is angry and hurt it has taken so long for her rescue, even though Rory irritably reminds her he waited 2,000 years for her (see *The Pandorica Opens*, 2010). Amy ultimately forgives Rory and The Doctor in favor of rescuing the Younger Amy from the timestream, which will cause her own death and erase her existence and nullify all of her actions and the exemplary courage she exhibited in this timestream for survival and persistence. Her courageous and loving action of self-sacrifice promotes the well-being of the relationship between the three of them and forgiveness releases her from the anxiety and hurt she has felt so keenly over many years.

Forgiveness is not only a process for individuals, but also has importance for societies and organizations. For instance, South Africa created a Truth and Reconciliation Commission after the dismantling of apartheid which was significant in moving the country forward. Through the loving actions of promoting overall well-being, a social system can begin to forgive, heal, and recover their unity. The critical understanding of forgiveness is not about the outcomes and repairing the relationship, but in the act of forgiving regardless of whether the wrongdoer makes amends or not. It is a process that primarily serves the one who has been injured and allows for their healing and ability to move forward.

In *Doctor Who*, we discover The Doctor wreaking havoc against some societies as a way to protect other societies, oftentimes the Earth. When cultures or civilizations are being attacked and their collapse seems imminent, it's not so easy to forgive. When people are experiencing the terror of impending death, "mortality salience engenders a greater need for death-denying cultural worldviews and consequently provokes more vigorous reactions to moral transgressors" (Solomon et al., 1998, p. 27). Those who have been repeatedly threatened with death or species extinction by The Doctor are understandably reluctant to forgive The Doctor and see them as an evildoer.

The Twelfth Doctor is called The Destroyer of Worlds by the Dalek creator, Davros, for his genocidal actions against the Daleks with their planet Skaro and the presumed destruction of the Time Lord planet, Gallifrey (*Journey's End*, 2008). The Doctor does not forgive the Daleks for their attack on Gallifrey and Davros does not forgive The Doctor for their repeated attacks against the Dalek forces. Davros continues to shame The Doctor for his actions in *The Magician's Apprentice* (2015), even though The Doctor had once taken pity on Davros as a child lost in a war-torn landscape, though ultimately abandoned him in a field of mines. The critical measure of forgiveness in *The Witch's Familiar* (2015), which continues this story of The Doctor and Davros, is The Doctor returning to the child Davros and leading him out of the mined battlefield. The child asks The Doctor which side of the war he is on. The Twelfth Doctor replies that it doesn't matter which side he is on as long as there is mercy. The Doctor has, in effect, forgiven the child Davros for the future destruction the Daleks will commit and throughout the rest of their encounters we witness the process of forgiveness – sometimes successful and sometimes not – as The Doctor comes to terms with the act of forgiving. For The Doctor, it is a courageous repeated action as they know there will be future encounters and a great deal of harm and destruction. But, particularly for the Twelfth Doctor, kindness is the significant action he is compelled to cultivate as a result of interactions with the Companions, and he must build the courage of acceptance for being kind.

REDEMPTION

Redemption is closely affiliated to forgiveness and is also a process that occurs through interaction by moving the participants from alienation to reconciliation (Clark, 2003). While forgiveness begins with a loving act of forgiving by the aggrieved person, redemption is a process beginning with the transgressor seeking forgiveness for his or her own actions. As with loving and forgiving, redemption is an action of personally improving and "honoring duties owed to oneself and to others... [with] an integrated change in one's actions or way of life that seeks to improve relationships with others, either individually or as members of a group" (Caldwell et al., 2011, p. 474). Unlike love and forgiveness, redemption is always a relational process and isn't an action that can be done alone, which is problematic for The Doctor who invariably retreats into the solitary sanctum of the TARDIS when they are struggling with difficult emotions such as regret and guilt.

It takes courage to seek redemption as there can always be a possibility of being denied forgiveness by the person or group that was wronged. It demands the transgressor be vulnerable and humble. The process can often start when someone is feeling most confused, afraid, or filled with shame and guilt. As Clark (2003) explains, "forgiveness must come out of confronting one's own feelings and belief systems. A person must let go of pride and be willing to accept the consequences of his or her actions" (p. 79).

For the Tenth Doctor, his moment of vulnerability and search for redemption begins as he starts to regenerate in *The End of Time, Part Two* (2010). Earlier, he has told Wilfred Mott, Donna Noble's grandfather and the Tenth Doctor's Companion for this episode, that he knows he is not innocent in terms of taking lives. He even admits that he has manipulated people into taking their own lives (see *Water of Mars*, 2009). But as he regenerates, he determines he will go "to get his reward" and offset the monstrous actions he has committed with good deeds (*The End of Time, Part Two*, 2010). He saves Martha Jones and Mickey Smith from being killed by a Sontaran. He slips a note to Captain Jack Harkness introducing him to Midshipman Alonzo Frame from the spaceship Titanic (see *The Voyage of the Damned*, 2007). He saves Sara Jane Smith's son, Luke, from being hit by a car. He drops into a book signing by Verity Newman, the great granddaughter of Joan Redfern whom he loved in the episodes *Human Nature* (2007) and *Family of Blood* (2007) to seek reassurance that Joan had a happy life. He then visits Wilfred Mott in the future and is told Donna Noble is getting married again. Donna still cannot know anything about The Doctor, but he gives Wilfred an envelope with a, presumably, winning lottery ticket as a wedding present. Finally, the Tenth Doctor visits Rose Tyler on New Year's Eve before she ever meets the Ninth Doctor or falls in love with him and is banished to a parallel universe, just to have a moment to see her again and tell her she is about to have a great year (*The End of Time, Part Two*, 2010).

These are all the moments where the Tenth Doctor attempts to redeem himself with acts of kindness toward the people he left behind. His vulnerability and fear in the moment before his death brings about feelings of shame and guilt that he is compelled to assuage before he regenerates. Importantly, these are moments of trying to repair his relationships with people he harmed in some way or another. It is an acknowledgement of his failings and his promise to do better. There is a sense that his actions were appreciated, and he has earned a bit of redemption, as the Ood appear to him and offer to sing him to his death (*The End of Time, Part Two*, 2010).

The Twelfth Doctor's story arc can be more clearly interpreted as exploring the process of redemption and the important courageous influence of his Companions in that process. In fact, the process begins almost from the very beginning of the Twelfth Doctor's arrival. Early in the episode *Deep Breath* (2014), The Doctor is scrounging in an alley absentmindedly in search of something. He catches an image of himself in a broken mirror and mumbles, "Why this one? Why did I choose this face? It's like I'm trying to tell myself something. Like I'm trying to make a point. But what is so important I can't just tell myself what I'm thinking?" The mention of his face refers to the episode *The Fires of Pompeii* (2008), where the Tenth Doctor saves a single family from the devastation of Mount Vesuvius erupting. Peter Capaldi played the father, Caecillius, in that episode and is now playing The Doctor. With this short piece of monologue, the story of the Twelfth Doctor is established as a search for learning a lesson that was once learned but must be learned again. The Doctor can't simply remind himself of the lesson of mercy, kindness, and compassion because, as a relational construct, it requires the courage of his Companions to also behave in forgiving ways as part of their healing process from being injured.

The next episode, *Into the Dalek* (2014), continues The Doctor questioning his moral integrity. The Twelfth Doctor asks Clara Oswald for an honest answer to the question of whether he is a good man. She is speechless for a moment, then answers that she doesn't know. This episode considers themes of kindness and compassion as they encounter an unusual Dalek that wants to kill other Daleks after witnessing the beautiful event of a star being born. The Doctor remarks, this is "morality as malfunction" (*Into the Dalek*, 2014). Clara becomes angry with The Doctor and challenges him to understand that the lesson they are learning is not that Daleks are evil, which only confirms The Doctor's prejudices, but that a good Dalek is possible. As the Twelfth Doctor enters the mind of the Dalek, the Dalek remarks that he sees much beauty, but ultimately the Dalek sees hatred and considers that to be good. In fact, he considers The Doctor to be a good Dalek because of his immense capacity for hatred. The Twelfth Doctor is anguished by this verdict (*Into the Dalek*, 2014).

At the end of the episode, Clara tells The Doctor she is not certain if he is a good man, but she knows he tries to be and that is the point. The Doctor replies that he believes her to be an amazing teacher (*Into the Dalek*, 2014). This dialogue helps to establish their relationship as complementary and more fully a mature partnership than their relationship in The Doctor's previous regeneration. The Doctor has lessons to learn about redemptive goodness and Clara is the courageous Companion who will help teach those lessons. In fact, Season 8 is filled with imagery of learning as The Doctor uses chalkboards and chalk – the archaic tools of teaching and learning – throughout.

Clara continues offering lessons in *Listen* (2014) as she meets The Doctor as a young boy who is crying in the dark. As mentioned above, being vulnerable and afraid can be a catalyst for change and the beginning of the process of redemption. Clara tells him "Fear is a superpower. Fear can make you faster and cleverer and stronger… Fear doesn't have to make you cruel or cowardly. Fear can make you kind…fear can bring us together" (*Listen*, 2014). Understanding that he will always be afraid and that it is okay to be afraid because there is a power in facing this fact and there is a force that brings together people who are afraid and can be transformed by kindness, allows The Doctor to eventually be able to seek redemption for the monstrous acts he has committed and the relationships he has neglected or destroyed.

Yet, when Missy, the next regeneration of his childhood friend and sociopathic nemesis The Master, tells the Twelfth Doctor they are not so different and she wants her friend back, the Twelfth Doctor realizes, "I am not a good man! I am not a bad man either! I am an idiot! Passing through. Helping out. Learning" (*Death in Heaven*, 2014). While Missy has offered him an army of Cybermen, he says he does not need an army because he has Companions and others who follow him. As he looks at Clara and her boyfriend, Danny Pink, who has been partially transformed into a Cyberman and has begged Clara to complete the conversion and end his pain, The Doctor states that love is not an emotion, but a promise (*Death in Heaven*, 2014). The Twelfth Doctor is learning the lesson of love as an action for the well-being of others.

The redemptive journey The Doctor takes must also pass through coming to terms with their purpose. For the Twelfth Doctor, this included understanding why he regenerated into the face he has, as seen in the episode *Deep Breath* (2014). In *The Girl Who Died* (2015), the Twelfth Doctor is racked with guilt over the death of a Viking girl, Ashildr, who he persuaded to be a part of his plan to defeat the alien forces of a warrior culture, the Mya. He laments out loud that he is "sick of losing people," as this death comes on the heels of the death of Danny Pink, Osgood, Amy and Rory, among the many others. He also knows he is not supposed to break the rules and bring someone back from the dead or change history in ways that destroy fixed events, like he did with Caecilius' family in *The Fires of Pompeii* (2008). Nevertheless, as he stares into a water barrel, like he stared into the mirror before in *Deep Breath* (2014), he learns why he has the face of Caecilius. It is "to remind me. To hold me to the mark. I'm The Doctor. And I save people" (*The Girl Who Died*, 2015). He brings Ashildr back to life through alien technology, though he also knows he might regret the act later and that she might not be appreciative of the gesture because it could make her immortal. Even so, he has solidified his purpose and mission by "honoring duties owed to oneself and to others" (Caldwell et al., 2011, p. 474), which not only strengthens his relationship with his Companions and other followers but allows him to move further down the path of redemption. He has learned the lesson of who he is and the actions he must take to be a "good man."

His newfound commitment to kindness and loving actions through honoring his duties as The Doctor are tested in the aftermath of Clara's death (*Face the Raven*, 2015; *Heaven Sent*, 2015; *Hell Bent*, 2015). As it is evident, Clara will not be saved from death, they both know the Twelfth Doctor will want to take revenge. She implores him not to. Clara takes her final moments to be courageous and thinks of the impact on others and how to prevent catastrophe. She tells The Doctor, "You're going to be alone and you're very bad at that... But listen to me, don't let this change you... I know what you're capable of. Don't be a warrior. Promise me. Be a doctor" (*Face the Raven*, 2015). Her unique skills as a Companion and being able to facilitate and reinforce The Doctor's learning are courageously demonstrated up to the moment of her death as she bravely goes to face the raven that will take her life.

But, of course, The Doctor does want revenge. There is no expectation that the process of forgiveness and redemption is linear and that there will not be moments when a person may backslide or lose their way. The Doctor's relationship with Clara was a strong mature partnership that thrived as Clara applied the courageous followership practices previously discussed. Her loss is a significant shock and creates his need for vengeance even though she specifically did not want him to regress to old destructive behaviors. In *Heaven Sent* (2015), The Doctor asks a silent ghost-like Clara standing at a chalkboard with her back to him what he is supposed to do. Her answer is written in chalk, "tell no lies." But we know that Rule #1 is "The Doctor lies." Her admonition is vitally important as The Doctor has been teleported by the Time Lords into his confession dial. The dial is meant to be an act of purification that allows a dying Time Lord the ability to face their demons and make their peace (*Hell Bent*, 2015). But it has been turned into a torture chamber for him and he must speak the truth to be released.

In *Heaven Sent* (2015), The Doctor truthfully admits to his fear of dying. The final truth he must share is his knowledge of The Hybrid, prophesied to be a destructive force against the Time Lords. But he refuses to tell the entire truth as he believes himself to be The Hybrid and does not want to face that or give away his knowledge to the Time Lords. He spends four billion years inside the confession dial, repeating a process of teleporting, eluding The Veil that is always tracking him, solving the mystery of his whereabouts, waiting for The Veil to catch up to him and mortally wound him, and endlessly chipping away at a wall of Azbantium, which is harder than diamond, with his bare hand until he breaks through and finds himself in Gallifrey ready to take his vengeance upon the Time Lords. While his experience in the confession dial is not his redemption, it is clearly his self-imposed penance.

Back on Gallifrey, he overcomes and banishes the Lord President, then hopes to redeem himself by saving Clara through a plan to snatch Clara from her timeline in the heartbeat before her death (*Hell Bent*, 2015). But Clara is not as grateful as he would have liked and insists that she should have the choice as to the manner and time of her death. The Doctor devises an instrument that should remove her memories of him, much as he did for Donna Noble (see *Journey's End*, 2008). But Clara is furious that he would even consider taking her memories of their time together away from her. She reverses the polarity so The Doctor's memories of her are erased. Neither knows if the adjustment worked and when they decide they will make one more reckless choice and see who will lose their memory, The Doctor loses, and he forgets Clara. But Clara still leaves him one more teachable moment with a chalkboard message of "Run you clever boy and be a doctor" (*Hell Bent*, 2015).

The Twelfth Doctor's journey of redemption continues after the loss of Clara's memory. His next Companions, Bill Potts, a young woman he chooses to mentor under his assumed identity as a university professor, and Nardole, a cyborg he met on Mendorax Dellora (see *The Husbands of River Song*, 2015), have several adventures before attempting to rehabilitate Missy into a good person in *World Enough and Time* (2017). The four of them teleport to a ship on the edge of a black hole. Due to the time differential being so close to the event horizon, the front of the 400-mile-long ship moves through time much slower than the back. While the sole remaining pilot thinks only a few days have passed, it has been centuries for those below. In the ensuing centuries, they have been creating Cybermen as an army to do the bidding of The Master who has been stranded on the ship decades prior due to a faulty TARDIS.

The Cybermen can sense human beings and they come for Bill Potts. The pilot believes they will leave her alone if she is dead and shoots her. Nevertheless, the primitive form of Cybermen arrive and take her away to be repaired. No one realizes the definition of being repaired is to be changed into a Cyberman, as their form is not immediately obvious and so the danger is not understood. After surgery, Bill does not realize she has been changed and still holds onto her humanity and emotions. Years later, the Twelfth Doctor finds her, but is taken captive by The Master and Missy. When they try to escape, Cyberman Bill prevents that and she and Nardole take The Doctor to a solar farm level to allow him to recuperate (*World Enough and Time*, 2017; *The Doctor Falls*, 2017).

The people on the solar farm level are wary and afraid of her, but Bill does not know why as she has yet to realize she is a Cyberman. Finally, a child brings her a mirror, and she discovers the truth which causes her tremendous heartache and denial. Interestingly, Bill is primarily seen as Bill during these episodes and less frequently as a Cyberman, especially by The Doctor. This choice echoes the Twelfth Doctor's distress when Clara refuses to see him as The Doctor in *Deep Breath* (2014) and the Twelfth Doctor's learning commitment to seeing the basic humanity and goodness in others beyond their outward appearance.

As they prepare to fight the Cybermen who are coming to the solar farm level to abduct the children and make them into Cybermen, Bill chooses to stay and fight with The Doctor as Nardole takes the children and some other adults to safety on a different level. The Twelfth Doctor enters the battle saying, "Without hope. Without witness. Without reward" (*The Doctor Falls*, 2017). He has no real intention to regenerate another time and expects he will die in this battle and that his sacrifice will redeem him. As the Cybermen close in, he takes his sonic screwdriver and blasts them all leaving a crater of desolation (*The Doctor Falls*, 2017).

Cyberman Bill has survived and finds The Doctor nearly lifeless in the midst of the battlefield. Even though she waited decades for him, and he could not save her from becoming a Cyberman, she sobs uncontrollably over his body. He was her friend and mentor, and she ostensibly forgives him for his shortcomings and grieves his loss. Just then, Heather, her crush who transmogrified into a fluid alien (see *The Pilot*, 2017), appears from a puddle of water and helps her leave her cyber body and into "a different kind of living" (*The Doctor Falls*, 2017). They take the Twelfth Doctor back to his TARDIS where they believe he belongs.

And yet, The Doctor's journey of redemption is still not over.

The TARDIS powers up and The Doctor finds himself at the South Pole and still refuses to regenerate. He shoves his regenerating hands into the snow-packed ground to stop the process, when he hears someone else say they refuse to change as well. It is the First Doctor. They have an awkward meeting, and inexplicably the snow stops falling and hangs in midair. Time has stopped. As they continue a clumsy and humorous dialogue, Twelfth Doctor finally declares, "Either we change and go on. Or we die as we are" (*Twice Upon a Time*, 2017). This is an important moment. Change is at the core of the leadership process. Without change, the status quo is preserved to the point where an organization – or a Time Lord – becomes stagnant and ceases to exist. It's an essential lesson to understand that change allows for persistence toward goals and fulfillment of purpose.

A captain from World War I suddenly appears as a result of the time streams between the two Doctors in the same place and time causing problems. The First Doctor is then transported into a ship by Professor Helen Clay, who presents as a computerized woman made of glass, and represents The Testimony, the future humans who take the memories of those who are about to die as testimony and history for future humans. They want the captain in trade for giving the Twelfth Doctor an opportunity to speak with Bill again. But the Twelfth Doctor refuses to believe the figure in front of him is Bill as she died as a Cyberman, and this makes her quite angry that he can no longer see her or her humanity. She insists her memories are what constitute her as her (*Twice Upon a Time*, 2017). The Twelfth Doctor is making it difficult for Bill to grant him redemption for his transgressions against her if he refuses to accept her in her current form.

The narrative returns to the question of being "a good man" as Professor Clay shows the First Doctor who he is to become and explains, "The Doctor has walked in blood through all of time and space" (*Twice Upon a Time*, 2017). The First Doctor talks with Bill and ponders why the Twelfth Doctor is concerned with the idea of goodness. "Good is not a practical survival strategy. It requires loyalty, self-sacrifice, and love. And so, why does good prevail? What keeps the balance between good and evil in this appalling universe?" Bill responds, "perhaps it's just a bloke" (*Twice Upon a Time*, 2017).

Eventually, they return the captain to his moment of death, but the Twelfth Doctor has manipulated the time and prevents his death by bringing him back just a few moments later than he should have when the Christmas Armistice occurred in 1914 and fighting stopped for a brief moment as each side celebrated Christmas with each other. The captain lives and The Doctor discovers he is Lethbridge-Stewart who creates UNIT and becomes a great friend of The Doctor (*Twice Upon a Time*, 2017).

The First Doctor chooses to regenerate, and the Twelfth Doctor must make his choice. Before Bill leaves, she gives him back his memories of Clara. The Twelfth Doctor realizes it is "time to leave the battlefield" and chooses regeneration. The Twelfth Doctor is finally moving toward the end of his redemptive process by letting go of his pride and accepting the vulnerability and ambiguity of becoming someone different. As he begins the process, he has some words of advice for his new self. "Never be cruel, never be cowardly, and never eat pears. Remember… hate is always foolish. Love is always wise. Always try to be nice, never fail to be kind. … . Laugh hard. Run fast. Be kind" (*Twice Upon a Time*, 2017).

What we find is The Doctor's journey of redemption culminates in the necessity to be kind, fulfill the full purpose of being a doctor, and to save people. This is what he accomplishes with the help of his courageous Companions who face the fear and obstacles with him and never stop loving, forgiving, teaching, and supporting. The role of the Companions in helping The Doctor to develop empathy, love, the capacity to forgive, and the desire to seek redemption is an important arc not only in the ongoing story of The Doctor, but also in the development of the Companions and their competence in demonstrating courageous behaviors in support of The Doctor and the furtherance of the mission and purpose. As their efforts impact the effectiveness of The Doctor and increase their own skills and qualities, the co-construction of the leadership process is deepened and the ability to achieve the mission and purpose they have set for themselves is realized in profound ways.

OTHERNESS

There is one more area of importance that should be examined beyond the courageous followership model identified in the previous chapters. As with most science fiction narratives, aliens are often defined as evil and are to be resisted, if not eliminated. Particularly for nonhuman otherness, we consider those who are not completely human "as scapegoat bearers of evil, [who] warrant domination, banishment, and death" (Solomon et al., 1998, p. 18).

While the shared purpose of The Doctor and Companions may be to protect Earth, this is often accomplished by creating the Otherness of Alien Evil and working to control, banish, or kill aliens. Daleks and Cybermen are most often identified as Evil Others in the *Doctor Who* series, but Weeping Angels, Slitheen, Martians, the Judoon, Sycorax, and many other alien species that populate the Whoniverse also fit into this category.

However, according to Kearney (2003), we need to be able to understand what constitutes evil before we can act against it while also acknowledging the emotional and hurtful circumstances surrounding the definition of Otherness and seeking forgiveness. "The more we learn and accept our others, the more we learn and accept about our own selves, and both are changed in ways that allow for lessening concepts of evil and increasing personal actualization and harmony" (Yost, 2014, p. 206).

Being able to learn about others and accept them as a means for learning about ourselves is seen in episodes such as *Planet of the Ood* (2014), *The Hungry Earth* (2010), *The Magician's Apprentice* (2015), *Orphan 55* (2020), and *Deep Breath* (2014) and helps us to further our understanding of the importance of courageous followership in confronting difference. The two-part story arc of *The Zygon Invasion* (2015) and *The Zygon Inversion* (2015) brings the concepts of rejecting otherness and courageous follower-ship to the forefront.

While The Osgoods – Petronella, Nova, Bonnie, and perhaps others – are not specifically Companions, they are "big fans" of The Doctor and can certainly be considered followers of them. We first meet Osgood in *The Day of the Doctor* (2013) as Kate Stewart's scientific officer at UNIT. We immediately know she is a follower of the Doctor as she wears a large colorful wool scarf similar to the one worn by the Fourth Doctor and fangirls when she meets the Eleventh Doctor. In this episode, shape-shifting Zygons infiltrate UNIT and duplicate the bodies of humans, including Osgood. The Three Doctors – The War Doctor, Tenth Doctor, and Eleventh Doctor – work together to bring about a truce between Zygons and humans and prevent nuclear disaster and genocide.

Years later, we learn more about the truce and how it has affected the Zygons. Twenty million Zygons have been resettled on Earth and appear as humans, living their lives in peace and harmony. But a faction of Zygons have begun to rebel against this and rise up against humans. Their leader states,

"We have been betrayed. We were sold. Our rights were violated. We demand the right to be ourselves. No more lies" (*The Zygon Invasion*, 2015).

A video shows us two Osgoods who are a part of Operation Double, a project outside of UNIT, which works toward maintaining the truce. (The Osgoods are still big fans as one wears a vest with question marks reminiscent of previous Doctor incarnations and the other has the large scarf like the Fourth Doctor and a bow tie in homage to the Eleventh Doctor.) The Osgoods have a box which they state is a final sanction in case the ceasefire fails. In the video they explain, "Every race is capable of the best and the worst. Every race is peaceful and warlike. Good and evil" (*The Zygon Invasion*, 2015). But their words are not heeded. The humans want to use a gas that will kill all the Zygons and the rogue Zygon leaders want to find the box to have the tactical advantage against the humans. They kidnap one of the Osgoods in order to find the box.

The Twelfth Doctor arrives and speaks to Kate Stewart. She tells him there have always been two Osgoods since the ceasefire and that she never knew which one was real. The Twelfth Doctor retorts, "Both of them...They were both Zygon and human at the same time. They not only administered the peace. They were the peace" (*The Zygon Invasion*, 2015). The Doctor clearly intends to make Kate Stewart aware that her casual prejudice against an alien species is not acceptable.

Even so, when The Doctor finds Osgood, he asks her whether she is the human or the Zygon. Osgood replies, "I don't answer that question... I don't accept it. My sister and I were the living embodiment of the peace we made. I am the peace. I am human and Zygon" (*The Zygon Invasion*, 2015). Osgood refuses to lend credence to the idea of Zygon Otherness and that Zygons are somehow lesser than humans and should be considered evil, dangerous, or not worthy of respect.

In *The Zygon Inversion* (2015), the Zygon Bonnie, who has duplicated the form of Clara Oswald and found the Osgood boxes, is insistent on fighting the humans because she believes they cannot accept the way Zygons really are. In the Black Archives, the Twelfth Doctor explains that the only way anyone can live in peace is if they are prepared to forgive and he forgives Bonnie. The lesson of forgiveness has become an important theme in The Doctor's story, not only for those Companions who will forgive them, but also for The Doctor's ability to forgive and turn away from their reputation as destroyers.

The crisis is averted, and the Twelfth Doctor erases the memories of everyone in the room, as he has done 15 times before when the truce was in danger of being breached. This time, he does not erase Zygon Bonnie's memories. She doesn't understand how The Doctor could forgive her and he replies that he has been where she is and relates the story of being the War Doctor and having to choose whether to destroy Gallifrey and the Daleks or not (see *The Day of the Doctor*, 2013).

Later, The Doctor invites Osgood to travel on the TARDIS, but she declines as she must stay to defend the Earth, fulfilling the role of followers of The Doctor. But the Twelfth Doctor can't resist asking her again as to whether she is the human or the Zygon. She replies, "I am Osgood. I'll answer that question one day. And do you know when that day will be?" Another Osgood, presumably the previous Zygon Bonnie now duplicating Osgood, appears behind her and answers, "The day nobody cares about the answer" (*The Zygon Inversion*, 2015).

These two episodes are important in our understanding of courageous followership and the co-construction of the leadership process. *Doctor Who* is filled with stories about dangerous, violent Others who seek to destroy whatever is in their path and must be defeated at any cost by The Doctor and Companions. There are stories about liberating oppressed beings, such as the Ood, and standing up for social justice, but the theme is not often turned toward humans on Earth in such an explicit way that challenges our prejudices and biases against those who are different. It reminds us that not every alien being is evil and we have a certain level of responsibility for our own evilness in creating the systemic structures and cultural norms that repress, if not subjugate, others. We can experience the hurtful circumstances of Otherness through the story of the rebel Zygons and also find a model for acknowledging duality and seeking forgiveness in the characters of Osgood. Refusing to be labeled as human or Other is a courageous act and Osgoods' dedication to The Doctor's mission of defending the Earth provides a lesson to all of us. We don't have to be Companions to be courageous followers of The Doctor.

SUMMARY

It takes extraordinary courage to find the ability to love, forgive, and seek redemption. Fear of rejection, incompetence, vulnerabilities, and other emotional issues can tie us to the status quo and prevent our personal development and persistence in the face of adversity. But our ability to co-construct a leadership process within the framework of being a mature partner to our leader depends on our ability to cultivate the well-being of others through loving actions, engage in the process of forgiveness – whether the person who wronged us is aware of our forgiving attitude or not – and participate in the process of redemption, either by facilitating redemption in the person who injured us or by honoring our responsibilities to ourselves and others through seeking redemption for ourselves. We must also be aware of how we set paradigms in our relationships with others that are hurtful because of using those who are different as reflections of our own intolerance.

REFLECTIVE ACTIVITIES

- Reflect upon a time when you acted in a loving way that was not prompted by a romantic feeling. When have you acted in a loving way that was an intentional sympathetic response for the well-being of others? Was this a moment of personal interaction with another person or persons, or something less so, such as donating to an emergency disaster relief fund? What emotions did you feel in the moments before, during, and after your actions? How might you develop the ability to establish a habit of loving actions for the well-being of others? How might you ensure your loving actions include interpersonal connections to others who might be strangers? How might you influence others to participate in loving actions at work, school, or in your community?

- How easily do you forgive others? Do you find yourself needing to go through the process of forgiveness every time you interact with them? How does this make you feel? If the transgressor is your boss or a peer, in what ways does this compromise your working relationship or ability to achieve objectives? What steps could you take to make sure your ability to forgive is strengthened in an emotionally healthy manner or that you do not remind others of how they harmed you?

- Reflect on an action you are not proud of and consider how you might redeem yourself for your actions. What steps will you take to change your behavior and honor your duty to yourself and others? How will you demonstrate this change to others? How will you feel if others don't forgive your mistake? What will you need to do to maintain your new behaviors even if they are not appreciated by others?

9

BECOMING A COURAGEOUS COMPANION

One of the joys of watching *Doctor Who* is seeing ordinary people have extraordinary adventures. Companions to The Doctor are people we might know. They could be people we work with or see at the grocery. They aren't superheroes and don't possess exceptional talents in science, art, or business. They are simply good people mustering the courage to take a risk and do what is right. While we may live vicariously through their journeys, they also inspire us to be better – more courageous – people in our lives and the space and time we inhabit.

My intention for this book was to help you look at followership and courage through a lens you may not have considered before. Followership is not being docile or just obeying orders but a critical element of the leadership process and a vital component to the effectiveness and success of an organization, group, or society. The previous chapters have explored through academic theories and examples from the television series how this can be accomplished. Each chapter offered reflective activities to help you think about your own practice as a follower and your own levels of courage in that endeavor.

The first step to becoming a courageous companion is to be open to your own personal growth and development by knowing yourself. It's important to be able to name your fears, triggers, ambitions, and desires. It's also important to understand how we relate to others through our level of empathy and social skills in developing networks that accomplish common goals. Understanding our inner selves can help us identify why we behave in the ways we behave. And if we don't like our behaviors, we are more capable of changing them when we know what they are and how they hamper our growth and development, either personally or in our careers. Personal growth requires the courage to change. Change can be difficult and cause fear and anxiety. By confronting one's fear through reflection and practicing mindfulness to develop our emotional intelligence skills, courage is cultivated.

Some of us can simply sit and be reflective with our thoughts about ourselves when we encounter some type of dissatisfaction. Others of us may need a more structured approach to self-reflection. This could include setting a time each day or each week for reflection. Reflection could be meditative alone or involve journaling our thoughts and feelings so we can go back and review them. Conversely, some people find it helpful to do a "brain dump" and write down thoughts and feelings but toss the paper afterward. Still others may find therapy or counseling helpful if they are experiencing difficulties in their self-knowledge journey that requires support and assistance from a professional. In the end, it doesn't matter what form your reflection takes as long as it is beneficial, and you can see positive results in your personal life or career.

Courageous companions take responsibility for the completion of goals through igniting their passion for the purpose and objectives, taking the initiative, and connecting their personal values to the cultural norms of the organization or society. If you find yourself in a situation where you feel you are dissatisfied or disconnected from the purpose of the organization, it's important to think about what actions you can take to move you to a place of engagement. Often, this requires intrinsic motivation, but there is also the option of building stronger relationships with your leader and peers to gain the benefit of their motivating energy. A courageous companion does not work alone but requires interpersonal relationships to be successful.

Of course, sometimes it is necessary to have the courage to break the rules in order to accomplish goals. While you should never act in ways that are unethical or illegal, being able to skirt the edges in service to the overall purpose and mission of the organization may become necessary if there is an obstacle. The key is to know you are serving the purpose and not breaking rules because it's easier than dealing with the bureaucracy or you just don't like the rules. You should never break the rules as a self-serving gesture, either. Courageousness can also entail working within the system to change the rules that are impediments to effectiveness or harmful to members of the organization or society.

The concept of followers as serving the leader is fairly ingrained in our beliefs, but there is a misconception that serving means being servile. This is far from the truth of courageous followership. In building a relationship with a leader that shares the responsibility of the leadership process for influencing others and accomplishing goals, being able to aid the leader is crucial. The courageous companion does this by building trust, communicating honestly and appropriately, and being careful about how much access you need to the leader and what you do with that access. Courageous followers don't seek out the leader to green light their every action. When there is a strong understanding of the goals and mutual trust, respect, and open communication with a leader, access can be limited. This will encourage high quality interactions when they happen. Maintenance of the relationship with a leader is important and can be accomplished through limited access and strong positive communications when other elements are in place. Positive communication could involve the current objectives, but could also be a time to check in with each other to take the temperature of how they are doing emotionally or physically.

Courageous companions must also defend the leader. Of course, it's unconscionable to defend a leader who is found to be corrupt or incompetent. The majority of leaders are not, yet organizations can be destroyed because a few people who are dissatisfied decide to voice unfounded opinions, and no one steps up to disagree. Defending a leader is not making excuses for their behavior or strategies, but engaging in positive conversations that can persuade others to a distinct perspective that may alter their view and bring about cohesion in the organization. Certainly, if rumors or dissent is left unchecked the possibility of accomplishing goals and fulfilling the mission and purpose is compromised.

That is not to say dissent should never be allowed. Followers must find the courage to challenge their leaders. I find this quote to be an important lesson: "The most capable followers in the world will fail if they gripe about their leaders but don't help them improve" (Chaleff, 2009, p. xix). Challenging the leader with evidence, compassion, professionalism, and honest feedback are all ways in which followers can courageously challenge their leaders and provide the opportunity for the leader to improve. This isn't easy, of course, so followers must be certain their relationship with the leader is strong and holds mutual respect. If a leader knows their follower is coming from a place of concern and seeks to make them better in the pursuit of common goals, it is easier for the follower to succeed.

Change is a constant in organizations and societies. Indeed, organizations and societies that fail to change can fail to exist. Courage is needed to meet the transformational changes in our workplaces and communities. Facing our fears about change and the ambiguity of an unknown future is a process where courage is imperative. Followers become important assets to the change process for influencing others on a level their leaders may not be able to manage. Advocating for change with one's peers in the break room over a cup of coffee can sometimes be more effective than a corporate memo or speech at a staff meeting. Followers are often positioned to actively listen in a way leaders may not be able to do with everyone in the hierarchy. Importantly, followers must then communicate concerns to the leader for them to be addressed. No, this does not mean snitching on your peers. Courageous followers present complaints and concerns in a professional reasonable manner that is consistent with being able to fashion a strong response to those concerns that serves the mission and accomplishes the goals without demeaning or embarrassing those who dissent.

Organizational transformation can also include the leader you have grown to admire, respect, and work well with may leave the organization. They transfer, retire, get downsized, or move on to another company. As a courageous follower, you will want to acknowledge there is a grieving process when this happens. You will go through multiple stages of change dealing with the loss of a leader and building a relationship with a new leader. This is a normal process, and you should allow it to take the time it needs. That said, don't belabor the process and wallow in grief. Look for the opportunities to demonstrate your courage and move through the stages and be ready to enter a new phase of your presence in the organization and your role as a courageous companion.

And yet, sometimes it is crucial for a follower to have the courage to oppose the leader. There may be situations where a leader asks for unethical or illegal actions. They may propose plans that are detrimental to people, the environment, or the well-being of the organization or society. In these instances, followers practice the courage of their convictions and have a duty to disobey. In an ideal situation, the duty to disobey is communicated openly and the follower can persuade the leader to a different course of action before any harm occurs. As you might imagine, this is exceedingly difficult. Courage is required to align the values of the organization with your personal values and refuse to act in ways that run counter to those values.

Followers may not be willing to advocate for policies or actions that are unethical, illegal, or imminently cause harm. They may find they must withdraw their support for their leader. In this instance, you may find it is beneficial to stay at the organization but be less present or engaged. Not everyone is able to simply quit a job or organization because they have a strong disagreement. But courageous followers can learn to quietly work within the system to repeal ill-conceived policies or mitigate the fallout of bad actions. There will be a process of grief in this situation, as well, because you lost the relationship and influence you worked hard to build. Remember there is always the potential to rebuild the relationship over time and correct the issues. The withdrawal of support does not mean you will never be able to give your support to the leader later. It may also mean that staying gives you the opportunity to build alternative relationships that can be effective and influential.

The most challenging situation is when you must physically leave. It takes courage to leave and is not an action to be taken lightly. There may be a time when you must leave on moral grounds, such as not being able to persuade your leader not to take an unethical or illegal action. But you may find the more typical reason for leaving is that you have outgrown where you are and your relationship with your leader. If you have been conscientious about personal development, opportunities may arise you were not expecting. A courageous follower who believes strongly in the purpose and modes of behavior they have built can take advantage of the new opportunities and be able to spread their courage to other places. Leaving with grace and dignity is always an optimal choice. You won't want to burn your bridges behind you as the relationships and influence you have already cultivated may prove useful in the future.

A fascinating outcome of my thinking about *Doctor Who* is the importance of love, forgiveness, and redemption in defining and practicing courageous companionship. It takes courage to overcome our fears to love, forgive, and seek redemption. We must learn to act intentionally with sympathy for the well-being of others. Loving actions can be hard because we might not want to demonstrate our vulnerability or we don't understand others as well as we should, especially if we consider them to be remarkably different from us. And yet, to be a courageous companion we must find the way to love as a way of influencing others toward common goals.

Forgiveness may take even more courage than love. Humans can harbor grudges and distrust of others for generations. Developing the courage to let go of our grievances and forgive others for their transgressions against us can liberate us from negative models of behavior and emotions. We don't have to confront the others to tell them we forgive them. In fact, each time we encounter someone who has hurt us we participate in an act of forgiving as we interact with them. It gets easier over time. The key understanding is followers must often forgive their leaders for not living up to the expectations we have and our relationship with them. It's not necessarily feasible to dispose of our leaders each time we are hurt by their words or actions, so we must develop the courage to forgive them and move forward to accomplish our common goals.

The process of redemption helps us to move from alienation to reconciliation in our relationships. Leaders may seek to be redeemed in the eyes of their followers, and the courageous follower should be open to the possibility of granting that redemption. It's not something the leader can do on their own. They need their follower(s) to be a part of the process and help them accomplish it when they are having difficulties. And they will invariably have difficulties. This courageous helping posture rebuilds the trust, respect, and mutual benefit of the relationship between the follower and leader.

Finally, courageous companions must be dedicated to embracing those who are designated as Other. By learning about Others and their experiences and challenges, we learn about ourselves and come to discover the common humanity we share. Challenging stereotypes, prejudices, biases, and disrespectful behaviors toward marginalized or oppressed people makes us better people and creates more effective and just organizations and societies. You may feel you are designated as an Other in your organization or society due to your race, ethnicity, faith, sexual orientation, gender identification, disability, geographic or national origin, age, educational level, or any other of the myriad ways humans have learned to categorize, discriminate, and demean fellow humans. Your courage as a follower to be a change agent and partner in generating social justice is vital to our organizations and societies.

It is my sincere hope you have gained some knowledge about the critical importance and level of courage required for followers in co-constructing the leadership process. As we see through the examples of the Companions and Doctors in *Doctor Who*, followers are not simply compliant or obedient, they don't need to become the leader to fulfill their personal growth, and they are not cowardly or lacking in authority, dignity, or value. Indeed, followers are indispensable, as the Courageous Companions aptly demonstrate.

As you travel the journey of courage in your own life...

Laugh hard.

Run fast.

Be kind.

(It's okay to eat the pears.)

Appendix 1

BRIEF DESCRIPTIONS OF COMPANIONS AND CHARACTERS

Character	Portrayed By	Brief Description
Ace (Dorothy)	Sophie Aldred	Originally a companion of the Seventh Doctor from Perivale, Ace returns to help UNIT and the Thirteenth Doctor fight The Master. She is known for carrying a baseball bat and being a chemistry whiz
Ashildr/Me	Miasie Williams	A Viking girl who dies in combat with the Mya and is brought back to life by the Twelfth Doctor, but she becomes immortal. She eventually turns against The Doctor
Clay, Helen	Nikki Amuka-Bird	Glass Woman of The Testimony
Cooper, Gwen	Eve Myles	A member of Torchwood who defends Earth from aliens with Jack Harkness and Ianto Jones
Davros	Julian Bleach	The creator of the Daleks
Flint, Jenny	Catrin Stewart	Wife of Madame Vastra and helps her and Strax investigate mysteries in Victorian London
Frame, Alonzo	Russell Tovey	Midshipman on the doomed spaceship Titanic who is one of the few survivors
Harkness, Captain Jack	John Barrowman	A rogue time traveler from the 51st Century who frequently crosses paths with The Doctor. Is given leadership of Torchwood
Heather	Stephanie Hyam	A woman abducted by an alien lifeform to be the pilot of their ship. She becomes a shape shifting watery substance able to travel across time and space. She falls in love with Bill Potts

(Continued)

(Continued)

Character	Portrayed By	Brief Description
Jones, Harriet	Penelope Winton	Jones is a House of Commons backbencher who helps the Ninth Doctor foil an alien invasion and becomes Prime Minister. Jones earns the wrath of the Tenth Doctor, resulting in losing her position. She ultimately saves Earth from the Daleks by sacrificing her own life
Jones, Ianto	Gareth David-Lloyd	A member of Torchwood who defends Earth from aliens with Jack Harkness and Gwen Cooper
Jones, Martha	Freema Agyeman	A medical student saved by the Tenth Doctor. Becomes a leader of UNIT. Marries Mickey Smith
Khan, Yasmin	Mandip Gill	A probationary officer from Sheffield and a primary school classmate of Ryan Sinclair who travels with the Thirteenth Doctor. She has romantic feelings for The Doctor, but they are not acted upon
Lewis, Dan	John Bishop	A Companion to the Thirteenth Doctor who was abducted by Lupari. He is from Liverpool and works at a food bank but pretends to be a tour guide at a local museum
Master, The	Derek Jacobi John Simm Michelle Gomez Sacha Dhawan	The Master/Missy is a childhood friend of The Doctor and also a Time Lord. A childhood trauma of staring into the time vortex warped their mind and they became sociopathic
Mott, Wilfred	Bernard Cribbins	Donna's grandfather who supports the Tenth Doctor through various actions on Earth
Nardole	Matt Lucas	A cyborg who serves River Song and then becomes a companion to the Twelfth Doctor
Noble, Donna	Catherine Tate	An outspoken temporary administrative assistant from Chiswick. Initially an accidental Companion, she gleefully travels with the Tenth Doctor. After taking in pure time energy and saving the universe, the Tenth Doctor erases her memories so she can return to her life on Earth
O'Brien, Graham	Bradley Walsh	A retiree and cancer survivor who loses his wife Grace to an alien attack. Becomes a companion to the Thirteenth Doctor. He is the step-grandfather to Ryan Sinclair
Osgoods	Ingrid Oliver	Scientific Advisor to UNIT who is a twin with a human/Zygon sister

(*Continued*)

Character	Portrayed By	Brief Description
Oswald, Clara	Jenna Coleman	Also known as The Impossible Girl, the character is shown to have followed The Doctor throughout the series. She is a Dalek, governess, and schoolteacher. Primarily the companion to the Eleventh and Twelfth Doctors
Pink, Danny (Rupert)	Samuel Anderson	Clara Oswald's boyfriend and fellow teacher at Coal Hill School. A former soldier in Afghanistan
Pond, Amy (Amelia)	Karen Gillan	Visited by the Eleventh Doctor as a child, she waits for him to return and becomes a Companion until she is disappeared by the Weeping Angels and dies in a different time and place
Potts, Bill	Pearl Mackie	A university cafeteria worker who becomes the Twelfth Doctor's Companion. She is "upgraded" to a Cyberman but maintains her humanity. She ultimately is given the ability to travel the universe with her girlfriend Heather
Sinclair, Ryan	Tosin Cole	A young man from Sheffield who travels with the Thirteenth Doctor. Step grandson to Graham O'Brien and school friend of Yasmin Khan
Smith, Mickey	Noel Clarke	Rose's boyfriend who also travels with the Ninth and Tenth Doctors. Becomes a freedom fighter in a parallel universe and marries Martha Jones
Smith, Sarah Jane	Elisabeth Sladen	Originally a Companion to the Third and Fourth Doctors, she meets up with the Tenth and Thirteenth Doctors to help save Earth again and again
Song, River	Alex Kingston	The daughter of Amy Pond and Rory Williams who becomes a time traveling archeologist and wife to The Doctor. Wrongly imprisoned for killing The Eleventh Doctor
Stewart, Kate	Jemma Redgrave	Head of UNIT
Strax	Dan Starkey	A Sontaran soldier and trained nurse relegated to living on Earth. Works with Madame Vastra and Jenny Flint to solve mysteries in Victorian London
Jovanka, Tegan	Janet Fielding	A former stewardess from Australia, she originally traveled with the Fourth and Fifth Doctors. She returns to help UNIT and the Thirteenth Doctor fight The Master
Tyler, Rose	Billie Piper	A shopgirl who travels with the Ninth and Tenth Doctors. She falls in love with them but is exiled to a parallel universe through a rift in space. She continues to fight Cybermen and returns to her original universe when the stars start to go out and she needs the help of the Tenth Doctor and Donna Noble

(*Continued*)

(Continued)

Character	Portrayed By	Brief Description
Vastra, Madame	Neve McIntosh	A homo reptilius lifeform saved by the Eleventh Doctor who now lives in Victorian London with her wife Jenny Flint and Strax. They investigate mysteries and watch over The Doctor
Williams, Brian	Mark Williams	Rory Williams' dad
Williams, Rory	Arthur Darvill	Husband to Amy Pond and Companion to the Eleventh Doctor until he is disappeared by the Weeping Angels and dies in a different time and place

The Doctors	Portrayed By	
Ninth Doctor	Christopher Eccleston	
Tenth Doctor/ Fourteenth Doctor	David Tennant	
Eleventh Doctor	Matt Smith	
Twelfth Doctor	Peter Capaldi	
Thirteenth Doctor	Jodie Whittaker	
The Fugitive Doctor	Jo Martin	
The War Doctor	John Hurt	
First Doctor	David Bradley	(Originally played by William Hartnell)

Appendix 2

EPISODE GUIDE

Episode Title	Airdate	Season/ Episode	Doctor(s)	Companion(s)
End of the World	4/2/2005	1.2	Ninth	Rose Tyler
The Unquiet Dead	4/9/2005	1.3	Ninth	Rose Tyler
World War Three	4/23/2005	1.5	Ninth	Rose Tyler
The Parting of the Ways	6/11/2005	1.13	Ninth	Rose Tyler
The Christmas Invasion	12/25/2005	2/Christmas Special	Tenth	Rose Tyler
Rise of the Cybermen	5/13/2006	2.5	Tenth	Rose Tyler Mickey Smith
Doomsday	7/8/2006	2.13	Tenth	Rose Tyler Mickey Smith Jackie Tyler Pete Tyler
The Runaway Bride	12/25/2006	3/Christmas Special	Tenth	Donna Noble
Smith and Jones	3/31/2007	3.1	Tenth	Martha Jones
The Shakespeare Code	4/7/2007	3.2	Tenth	Martha Jones
Gridlock	4/17/2007	3.3	Tenth	Martha Jones
Daleks in Manhattan	4/21/2007	3.4	Tenth	Martha Jones
The Lazarus Experiment	5/5/2007	3.6	Tenth	Martha Jones
Human Nature	5/26/2007	3.8	Tenth	Martha Jones
The Family Blood	6/2/2007	3.9	Tenth	Martha Jones

(Continued)

(*Continued*)

Episode Title	Airdate	Season/ Episode	Doctor(s)	Companion(s)
Blink	6/9/2007	3.10	Tenth	Martha Jones
The Last of the Time Lords	6/30/2007	3.13	Tenth	Martha Jones Jack Harkness
The Voyage of the Damned	12/25/2007	4/Christmas Special	Tenth	n/a
Partners in Crime	4/5/2008	4.1	Tenth	Donna Noble
Planet of the Ood	4/19/2008	4.2	Tenth	Donna Noble
The Fires of Pompeii	4/21/2008	4.2	Tenth	Donna Noble
The Sontaran Stratagem	4/26/2008	4.4	Tenth	Donna Noble Martha Jones
The Poison Sky	5/3/2008	4.5	Tenth	Donna Noble Martha Jones
Forest of the Dead	6/7/2008	4.9	Tenth	Donna Noble River Song
Turn Left	6/21/2008	4.11	Tenth	Donna Noble
The Stolen Earth	6/28/2008	4.12	Tenth	Donna Noble Rose Tyler Harriet Jones Sarah Jane Smith Martha Jones Jack Harkness Gwen Cooper Ianto Jones Wilfred Mott Mickey Smith Jackie Tyler
Journey's End	7/5/2008	4.13	Tenth	Donna Noble Rose Tyler Harriet Jones Sarah Jane Smith Martha Jones Jack Harkness Gwen Cooper Ianto Jones Wilfred Mott Mickey Smith Jackie Tyler
The Waters of Mars	11/15/2008	4.16	Tenth	n/a
The End of Time, Part Two	1/1/2010	4.18	Tenth	Wilfred Mott

(*Continued*)

Episode Title	Airdate	Season/ Episode	Doctor(s)	Companion(s)
The Beast Below	4/3/2010	5.1	Eleventh	Amy Pond
The Time of the Angels	4/24/2010	5.4	Eleventh	Amy Pond River Song
The Vampires of Venice	5/8/2010	5.6	Eleventh	Amy Pond Rory Williams
The Hungry Earth	5/22/2010	5.8	Eleventh	Amy Pond Rory Williams
Cold Blood	5/29/2010	5.9	Eleventh	Amy Pond Rory Williams
The Pandorica Opens	6/19/2010	5.12	Eleventh	Amy Pond Rory Williams River Song
The Big Bang	6/26/2010	5.13	Eleventh	Amy Pond Rory Williams River Song
A Good Man Goes to War	6/4/2011	6.7	Eleventh	Amy Pond Rory Williams River Song
The Girl Who Waited	9/10/2011	6.10	Eleventh	Amy Pond Rory Williams
Asylum of the Daleks	9/1/2012	7.1	Eleventh	Amy Pond Rory Williams Clara [Dalek]
Dinosaurs on a Spaceship	9/8/2012	7.2	Eleventh	Amy Pond Rory Williams Brian Williams
The Power of Three	9/22/2012	7.4	Eleventh	Amy Pond Rory Williams Brian Williams
The Snowmen	12/25/2012	7/Christmas Special	Eleventh	Clara [Governess]
The Name of the Doctor	5/18/2013	7.13	Eleventh Tenth War Doctor	Clara Oswald
The Day of the Doctor	11/23/2013	7/50th Anniversary	Eleventh Tenth War Doctor	Clara Oswald Rose Tyler Osgood

(Continued)

(Continued)

Episode Title	Airdate	Season/Episode	Doctor(s)	Companion(s)
Deep Breath	8/23/2014	8.1	Twelfth	Clara Oswald Madame Vastra Jenny Flint Strax
Into the Dalek	8/30/2014	8.2	Twelfth	Clara Oswald
Listen	9/13/2014	8.4	Twelfth	Clara Oswald
Kill the Moon	10/4/2014	8.7	Twelfth	Clara Oswald
Mummy on the Orient Express	10/11/2014	8.8	Twelfth	Clara Oswald
Death in Heaven	11/8/2014	8.12	Twelfth	Clara Oswald
The Magician's Apprentice	9/19/2015	9.1	Twelfth	Clara Oswald
The Witch's Familiar	9/26/2015	9.2	Twelfth	Clara Oswald
Under the Lake	10/3/2015	9.3	Twelfth	Clara Oswald
The Girl Who Died	10/17/2015	9.5	Twelfth	Clara Oswald
The Woman Who Lived	10/24/2015	9.6	Twelfth	Clara Oswald
The Zygon Invasion	10/31/2015	9.7	Twelfth	Clara Oswald Osgood
The Zygon Inversion	11/7/2015	9.8	Twelfth	Clara Oswald Osgood
Face the Raven	11/21/2015	9.10	Twelfth	Clara Oswald
Heaven Sent	11/28/2015	9.11	Twelfth	Clara Oswald
Hell Bent	12/5/2015	9.12	Twelfth	Clara Oswald
The Husbands of River Song	12/25/2015	9/Christmas Special	Twelfth	River Song
The Pilot	4/15/2017	10.1	Twelfth	Bill Potts
World Enough and Time	6/24/2017	10.11	Twelfth	Bill Potts Nardole
The Doctor Falls	7/1/2017	10.12	Twelfth	Bill Potts Nardole
Twice Upon a Time	12/25/2017	10/Christmas Special	Twelfth First	Bill Potts
Arachnids in the UK	10/28/2018	11.4	Thirteenth	Yasmin Khan Graham O'Brien Ryan Sinclair

(*Continued*)

Episode Title	Airdate	Season/Episode	Doctor(s)	Companion(s)
Orphan 55	1/12/2020	12.3	Thirteenth	Yasmin Khan Graham O'Brien Ryan Sinclair
Praxeus	2/2/2020	12.6	Thirteenth	Yasmin Khan Graham O'Brien Ryan Sinclair
Can You Hear Me?	2/9/2020	12.7	Thirteenth	Yasmin Khan Graham O'Brien Ryan Sinclair
Ascension of the Cybermen	2/23/2020	12.9	Thirteenth	Yasmin Khan Graham O'Brien Ryan Sinclair
Revolution of the Daleks	1/1/2021	12/Special	Thirteenth	Yasmin Khan Graham O'Brien Ryan Sinclair Jack Harkness
The Halloween Apocalypse	10/31/2021	13.1	Thirteenth	Yasmin Khan Dan Lewis
Survivors of the Flux	11/28/2021	13.5	Thirteenth	Yasmin Khan Dan Lewis
The Vanquishers	12/5/2021	13.6	Thirteenth	Yasmin Khan Dan Lewis
The Power of the Doctor	10/23/2022	13/Special	Thirteenth	Yasmin Khan Dan Lewis Ace Tegan Jovanka

REFERENCES

Barnes, D. F. (1978). Charisma and religious leadership: An historical analysis. *Journal for the Scientific Study of Religion, 17*(1), 1–18.

Berger, C. (2023, February 2). America is failing to prepare Gen Z to enter the workforce due to a 'glaring' gap in tech skills. *Fortune.* https://fortune.com/2023/02/02/gen-z-tech-skills-gap-workplace/

Block, P., & Burnett Heyes, S. (2022). Sharing the load: Contagion and tolerance of mood in social networks. *Emotion, 22*(6), 1193–1207.

Brown, B. (2018). *Dare to lead.* Random House.

Brown, C., White, R., & Kelly, A. (2021). Teachers as educational change agents: What do we currently know? Findings from a systematic review. *Emerald Open Research.* https://emeraldopenresearch.com/articles/3-26/v1

Caldwell, C., Dixon, R. D., Atkins, R., & Dowdell, S. M. (2011). Repentance and continuous improvement: Ethical implications for the modern leader. *Journal of Business Ethics, 102*, 473–487.

Campbell, J. (1949). *The hero with a thousand faces.* Princeton University Press.

Chaleff, I. (2009). *The courageous follower: Standing up to and for our leaders* (3rd ed.). Berrett-Koehler.

Chibnall, C. (Writer), & Aprahamian, S. (Director). (2018, October 28). Arachnids in the UK (Season 11, Episode 4) [TV series episode]. In C. Chibnall, M. Strevens, & S. Hoyle (Executive Producers), *Doctor Who.* BBC.

Chibnall, C. (Writer), & Janes, J. H. (Director). (2021, January 1). Revolution of the Daleks (Season 12, Festive Special) [TV series episode]. In C. Chibnall & M. Strevens (Executive Producers), *Doctor Who.* BBC.

Chibnall, C. (Writer), & Mackinnon, D. (Director). (2012, September 22). The Power of Three (Season 7, Episode 4) [TV series episode]. In S. Moffat & C. Skinner (Executive Producers), *Doctor Who.* BBC.

Chibnall, C. (Writer), & Metzstein, S. (Director). (2012, September 8). Dinosaurs on a Spaceship (Season 7, Episode 2) [TV series episode]. In S. Moffat & C. Skinner (Executive Producers), *Doctor Who.* BBC.

Chibnall, C. (Writer), & Saleem, A. (Director). (2021, December 5). The Vanquishers (Season 13, Episode 6) [TV series episode]. In C. Chibnall, M. Strevens, & N. Wilson (Executive Producers), *Doctor Who*. BBC.

Chibnall, C. (Writer), & Saleem, A. (Director). (2021, November 28). Survivors of the Flux (Season 13, Episode 5) [TV series episode]. In C. Chibnall, M. Strevens, & N. Wilson (Executive Producers), *Doctor Who*. BBC.

Chibnall, C. (Writer), & Stone, J. M. (Director). (2020, February 2). Praxeus (Season 12, Episode 6) [TV series episode]. In C. Chibnall & M. Strevens (Executive Producers), *Doctor Who*. BBC.

Chibnall, C. (Writer), & Stone, J. M. (Director). (2020, February 23). Ascension of the Cybermen (Season 12, Episode 9) [TV series episode]. In C. Chibnall & M. Strevens (Executive Producers), *Doctor Who*. BBC.

Chibnall, C. (Writer), & Stone, J. M. (Director). (2021, October 31). The Halloween Apocalypse (Season 13, Episode 1) [TV series episode]. In C. Chibnall, M. Strevens, & N. Wilson (Executive Producers), *Doctor Who*. BBC.

Chibnall, C. (Writer), & Stone, J. M. (Director). (2022, October 23). The Power of The Doctor (Season 13, Special) [TV series episode]. In C. Chibnall, M. Strevens, & N. Wilson (Executive Producers), *Doctor Who*. BBC.

Chibnall, C. (Writer), & Way, A. (Director). (2010, May 22). The Hungry Earth (Season 5, Episode 8) [TV Series episode]. In S. Moffat, P. Wenger, & B. Willis (Executive Producers), *Doctor Who*. BBC.

Chibnall, C. (Writer), & Way, A. (Director). (2010, May 29). Cold Blood (Season 5, Episode 9) [TV series episode]. In S. Moffat, P. Wenger, & B. Willis (Executive Producers), *Doctor Who*. BBC.

Clark, M. W. (2003). Redemption: Becoming more human. *The Expository Times*, *115*(76), 76–81.

Cornell, P. (Writer), & Palmer, C. (Director). (2007, June 2). The Family Blood (Season 3, Episode 9) [TV series episode]. In R. T. Davies & J. Gardner (Executive Producers), *Doctor Who*. BBC.

Cornell, P. (Writer), & Palmer, C. (Director). (2007, May 26). Human Nature (Season 3, Episode 8) [TV series episode]. In R. T. Davies & J. Gardner (Executive Producers), *Doctor Who*. BBC.

Dansereau, F., Graen, G. B., & Haga, W. (1975). A vertical dyad approach to leadership in formal organizations. *Organizational Behavior & Human Performance*, *13*, 46–78.

Davies, R. T. (Writer), & Ahearne, J. (Director). (2005, June 11). The Parting of the Ways (Season 2, Episode 13) [TV series episode]. In R. T. Davies, J. Gardner, & M. Young (Executive Producers), *Doctor Who*. BBC.

Davies, R. T. (Writer), & Boak, K. (Director). (2005, April 23). World War Three (Season 1, Episode 5) [TV series episode]. In R. T. Davies & J. Gardner (Executive Producers), *Doctor Who*. BBC.

Davies, R. T. (Writer), & Clark, R. (Director). (2007, April 14). Gridlock (Season 3, Episode 3) [TV series episode]. In R. T. Davies & J. Gardner (Executive Producers), *Doctor Who*. BBC.

Davies, R. T., Ford, P. (Writers), & Harper, G. (Director). (2009, November 15). The Waters of Mars (Season 4, Episode 16) [TV series episode]. In R. T. Davies & J. Gardner (Executive Producers), *Doctor Who*. BBC.

Davies, R. T. (Writer), & Harper, G. (Director). (2006, July 8). Doomsday (Season 2, Episode 13) [TV series episode]. In R. T. Davies & J. Gardner (Executive Producers), *Doctor Who*. BBC.

Davies, R. T. (Writer), & Harper, G. (Director). (2008, June 21). Turn Left (Season 4, Episode 11) [TV series episode]. In R. T. Davies & J. Gardner (Executive Producers), *Doctor Who*. BBC.

Davies, R. T. (Writer), & Harper, G. (Director). (2008, June 28). The Stolen Earth (Season 4, Episode 12) [TV series episode]. In R. T. Davies & J. Gardner (Executive Producers), *Doctor Who*. BBC.

Davies, R. T. (Writer), & Harper, G. (Director). (2008, July 5). Journey's End (Season 4, Episode 13) [TV series episode]. In R. T. Davies & J. Gardner (Executive Producers), *Doctor Who*. BBC.

Davies, R. T. (Writer), & Hawes, J. (Director). (2005, December 25). The Christmas Invasion (Season 2, Christmas Special) [TV series episode]. In R. T. Davies, J. Gardner, & M. Young (Executive Producers), *Doctor Who*. BBC.

Davies, R. T. (Writer), & Lyn, E. (Director). (2005, April 2). End of the World (Season 1, Episode 2) [TV series episode]. In R. T. Davies, J. Gardner, & M. Young (Executive Producers), *Doctor Who*. BBC.

Davies, R. T. (Writer), & Lyn, E. (Director). (2006, December 25). The Runaway Bride (Season 3, Christmas Special) [TV series episode]. In R. T. Davies, J. Gardner, & M. Young (Executive Producers), *Doctor Who*. BBC.

Davies, R. T. (Writer), & Lyn, E. (Director). (2010, January 1). The End of Time, Part Two (Season 4, Episode 18) [TV series episode]. In R. T. Davies & J. Gardner (Executive Producers), *Doctor Who*. BBC.

Davies, R. T. (Writer), & Palmer, C. (Director). (2007, March 31). Smith and Jones (Season 3, Episode 1) [TV series episode]. In R. T. Davies & J. Gardner (Executive Producers), *Doctor Who*. BBC.

Davies, R. T. (Writers), & Strong, J. (Director). (2007, December 25). The Voyage of the Damned (Season 4, Christmas Special) [TV series episode]. In R. T. Davies & J. Gardner (Executive Producers), *Doctor Who*. BBC.

Davies, R. T. (Writer), & Strong, J., (Director). (2008, April 5). Partners in Crime (Season 4, Episode 1) [TV series episode]. In R. T. Davies & J. Gardner (Executive Producers), *Doctor Who*. BBC.

Davies, R. T. (Writer), & Teague, C. (Director). (2007, June 30). The Last of the Time Lords (Season 3, Episode 13) [TV series episode]. In R. T. Davies & J. Gardner (Executive Producers), *Doctor Who*. BBC.

Dollard, S. (Writer), & Molotnikov, J. (Director). (2015, November 21). Face the Raven (Season 9, Episode 10) [TV series episode]. In S. Moffat & B. Minchin (Executive Producers), *Doctor Who*. BBC.

Elisabeth Kübler-Ross Foundation. (2023). Kübler-Ross change curve. https://www.ekrfoundation.org/5-stages-of-grief/change-curve/

Fiedler, F. E. (1964). A contingency model of leader effectiveness. *Advances in Experimental Social Psychology, 1*, 149–190.

Ford, P. (Writer), & Wheatley, B. (Director). (2014, August 30). Into the Dalek (Season 8, Episode 2) [TV series episode]. In S. Moffat & B. Minchin (Executive Producers), *Doctor Who*. BBC.

Gatiss, M. (Writer), & Lyn, E. (Director). (2005, April 9). The Unquiet Dead (Season 1, Episode 3) [TV series episode]. In R. T. Davies, J. Gardner, & M. Young (Executive Producers), *Doctor Who*. BBC.

Goleman, D. (2014). *What makes a leader: Why emotional intelligence matters*. More Than Sound.

Graen, G. B., & Uhl-Bien, M. (1995). Relationship-based approach to leadership: Development of leader-member exchange (LMX) theory of leadership over 25 years: Applying a multi-level, multi-domain perspective. *The Leadership Quarterly, 6*(2), 219–247.

Greenhorn, S. (Writer), & Clark, R. (Director). (2007, May 5). The Lazarus Experiment (Season 3, Episode 6) [TV series episode]. In R. T. Davies & J. Gardner (Executive Producers), *Doctor Who*. BBC.

Hamlin, A., Jr. (2016). *Embracing leadership: How to thrive in a leader-centric culture*. Kirkdale Press.

Harness, P. (Writer), & Nettheim, D. (Director). (2015, October 31). The Zygon Invasion (Season 9, Episode 7) [TV series episode]. In S. Moffat & B. Minchin (Executive Producers), *Doctor Who*. BBC.

Harness, P. (Writer), & Nettheim, D. (Director). (2015, November 7). The Zygon Inversion (Season 9, Episode 8) [TV series episode]. In S. Moffat & B. Minchin (Executive Producers), *Doctor Who*. BBC.

Harness, P. (Writer), & Wilmshurst, P. (Director). (2014, October 4). Kill the Moon (Season 8, Episode 7) [TV series episode]. In S. Moffat & B. Minchin (Executive Producers), *Doctor Who*. BBC.

Hime, E. (Writer), & Jones, L. H. (Director). (2020, January 12). Orphan 55 (Series 12, Episode 3) [TV series episode]. In C. Chibnall & M. Strevens (Executive Producers), *Doctor Who*. BBC.

Huczynski, A., & Buchanan, D. (2004). Theory from fiction: A narrative process perspective on the pedagogical use of feature film. *Journal of Management Education*, *28*(6), 707–726.

Inderjeet, A., & Scheepers, C. B. (2022). The influence of follower orientation on follower behavior in the leadership process. *SA Journal of Human Resource Management*, *20*.

James, C., Chibnall, C. (Writers), & Sullivan, E. (Director). (2020, February 9). Can You Hear Me? (Season 12, Episode 7) [TV series episode]. In C. Chibnall & M. Strevens (Executive Producers), *Doctor Who*. BBC.

Jiang, X., Snyder, K., Li, J., & Manz, C. C. (2021). Followers create leaders: The impact of effective followership on leader emergence in self-managing teams. *Group Dynamics: Theory, Research, and Practice*, *25*(4), 303–318.

Johnson, W. B. (2003). A framework for conceptualizing competence to mentor. *Ethics & Behavior*, *13*(2), 127–151.

Kateb, G. (2004). Courage as virtue. *Social Research*, *71*(1), 39–72.

Kearney, R. (2003). *Strangers, gods, and monsters*. Routledge.

Kegan, R., & Lahey, L. L. (2009). *Immunity to change: How to overcome it and unlock the potential in yourself and your organization*. Harvard Business Press.

Kellerman, B. (2007). What every leader needs to know about followers. *Harvard Business Review*, *85*(12), 84–91.

Kelley, R. E. (1992). *The power of followership: How to create leaders people want to follow and followers who lead themselves*. Doubleday.

King, U. (2004). Theories of love: Sorokin, Teilhard, and Tillich. *Zygon*, *39*(1), 77–102.

Kotter, J. P. (2001). What leaders really do [reprint]. *Harvard Business Review*, *79*(11), 85–97.

Lewis, D., Rodgers, D., & Woolcock, M. (2008). The fiction of development: Literary representations as a source of authoritative knowledge. *Journal of Development Studies*, *44*(2), 198–216.

MacRae, T. (Writer), & Harper, G. (Director). (2006, May 13). Rise of the Cybermen (Season 2, Episode 5) [TV series episode]. In R. T. Davies & J. Gardner (Executive Producers), *Doctor Who*. BBC.

MacRae, T. (Writer), & Hurran, N. (Director). (2011, September 10). The Girl Who Waited (Season 2, Episode 10) [TV series episode]. In S. Moffat, P. Wenger, & B. Willis (Executive Producers), *Doctor Who*. BBC.

Madsen, S. R., Gygi, J., Hammond, S. C., & Plowman, S. F. (2009). Forgiveness as a workplace intervention: The literature and a proposed framework. *Journal of Behavioral and Applied Management, 10*(2), 246–262.

Mathieson, J., Moffat, S. (Writers), & Bazalgette, E. (Director). (2015, October 17). The Girl Who Died (Season 9, Episode 5) [TV series episode]. In S. Moffat & B. Minchin (Executive Producers), *Doctor Who*. BBC.

Mathieson, J. (Writer), & Wilmshurst, P. (Director). (2014, October 11). Mummy on the Orient Express (Season 8, Episode 8) [TV series episode]. In S. Moffat & B. Minchin (Executive Producers), *Doctor Who*. BBC.

Matshoba-Ramuedzisi, T., de Jongh, D., & Fourie, W. (2022). Followership: A review of current and emerging research. *The Leadership & Organization Development Journal, 43*(4), 653–668. https://www.emerald.com/insight/publication/issn/0143-7739

Meyerson, D. E. (2003). *Tempered radicals: How everyday leaders inspire change at work*. Harvard Business School Press.

Moffat, S. (Writer), & Gough, L. (Director). (2017, April 15). The Pilot (Season 10, Episode 1) [TV series episode]. In S. Moffat & B. Minchin (Executive Producers), *Doctor Who*. BBC.

Moffat, S. (Writer), & Haynes, T. (Director). (2010, June 19). The Pandorica Opens (Season 5, Episode 12) [TV series episode]. In S. Moffat, P. Wenger, & B. Willis (Executive Producers), *Doctor Who*. BBC.

Moffat, S. (Writer), & Haynes, T. (Director). (2010, June 26). The Big Bang (Season 5, Episode 13) [TV series episode]. In S. Moffat, P. Wenger, & B. Willis (Executive Producers), *Doctor Who*. BBC.

Moffat, S. (Writer), & Hoar, P. (Director). (2011, June 4). A Good Man Goes to War (Season 6, Episode 7) [TV series episode]. In S. Moffat, P. Wenger, & B. Willis (Executive Producers), *Doctor Who*. BBC.

Moffat, S. (Writer), & Hurran, N. (Director). (2012, September 1). Asylum of the Daleks (Season 7, Episode 1) [TV series episode]. In S. Moffat & C. Skinner (Executive Producers), *Doctor Who*. BBC.

Moffat, S. (Writer), & Hurran, N. (Director). (2013, November 23). The Day of the Doctor (Season 7, 50th Anniversary Special) [TV series episode]. In S. Moffat & F. Penhale (Executive Producers), *Doctor Who*. BBC.

Moffat, S. (Writer), & Lyn, E. (Director). (2008, June 7). Forest of the Dead (Season 4, Episode 9) [TV series episode]. In R. T. Davies & J. Gardner (Executive Producers), *Doctor Who*. BBC.

Moffat, S. (Writer), & MacDonald, H. (Director). (2007, June 9). Blink (Season 3, Episode 10) [TV series episode]. In R. T. Davies & J. Gardner (Executive Producers), *Doctor Who*. BBC.

Moffat, S. (Writer), & MacDonald, H. (Director). (2015, September 19). The Magician's Apprentice (Season 9, Episode 1) [TV series episode]. In S. Moffat & B. Minchin (Executive Producers), *Doctor Who*. BBC.

Moffat, S. (Writer), & MacDonald, H. (Director). (2015, September 26). The Witch's Familiar (Season 9, Episode 2) [TV series episode]. In S. Moffat & B. Minchin (Executive Producers), *Doctor Who*. BBC.

Moffat, S. (Writer), & Mackinnon, D. (Director). (2014, September 13). Listen (Series 8, Episode 4) [TV series episode]. In S. Moffat & B. Minchin (Executive Producers), *Doctor Who*. BBC.

Moffat, S. (Writer), & Mackinnon, D. (Director). (2015, December 25). The Husbands of River Song (Series 9, Christmas Special). [TV series episode]. In S. Moffat & B. Minchin (Executive Producers), *Doctor Who*. BBC.

Moffat, S. (Writer), & Metzstein, S. (Director). (2012, December 25). The Snowmen (Season 7, Christmas Special) [TV series episode]. In S. Moffat & C. Skinner (Executive Producers), *Doctor Who*. BBC.

Moffat, S. (Writer), & Metzstein, S. (Director). (2013, May 18). The Name of the Doctor (Season 7, Episode 13) [TV series episode]. In S. Moffat & C. Skinner (Executive Producers), *Doctor Who*. BBC.

Moffat, S. (Writer), & Smith, A. (Director). (2010, April 24). The Time of Angels (Season 5, Episode 4) [TV series episode]. In S. Moffat, P. Wenger, & B. Willis (Executive Producers), *Doctor Who*. BBC.

Moffat, S. (Writer), & Smith, A. (Director). (2010, April 3). The Beast Below (Season 5, Episode 1) [TV series episode]. In S. Moffat, P. Wenger, & B. Willis (Executive Producers), *Doctor Who*. BBC.

Moffat, S. (Writer), & Talalay, R. (Director). (2017, July 1). The Doctor Falls (Series 10, Episode 12). [TV series episode]. In S. Moffat & B. Minchin (Executive Producers), *Doctor Who*. BBC.

Moffat, S. (Writer), & Talalay, R. (Director). (2014, November 8). Death in Heaven (Series 8, Episode 12). [TV series episode]. In S. Moffat & B. Minchin (Executive Producers), *Doctor Who*. BBC.

Moffat, S. (Writer), & Talalay, R. (Director). (2015, December 5). Hell Bent (Series 9, Episode 12). [TV series episode]. In S. Moffat & B. Minchin (Executive Producers), *Doctor Who*. BBC.

Moffat, S. (Writer), & Talalay, R. (Director). (2015, November 28). Heaven Sent (Series 9, Episode 11). [TV series episode]. In S. Moffat & B. Minchin (Executive Producers), *Doctor Who*. BBC.

Moffat, S. (Writer), & Talalay, R. (Director). (2017, December 25). Twice Upon a Time (Series 10, Christmas Special). [TV series episode]. In S. Moffat & B. Minchin (Executive Producers), *Doctor Who*. BBC.

Moffat, S. (Writer), & Talalay, R. (Director). (2017, June 24). World Enough and Time (Series 10, Episode 11). [TV series episode]. In S. Moffat & B. Minchin (Executive Producers), *Doctor Who*. BBC.

Moffat, S. (Writer), & Wheatley, B. (Director). (2014, August 23). Deep Breath (Season 8, Episode 1) [TV series episode]. In S. Moffat & B. Minchin (Executive Producers), *Doctor Who*. BBC.

Moran, J. (Writer), & Teague, C. (Director). (2008, April 21). The Fires of Pompeii (Season 4, Episode 2) [TV series episode]. In R. T. Davies & J. Gardner (Executive Producers), *Doctor Who*. BBC.

Northouse, P. G. (2019). *Leadership theory and practice* (8th ed.). Sage.

Oord, T. J. (2010). *Defining love: A philosophical, scientific, and theological engagement*. Brazos Press.

Pombeni, P. (2008). Charismatic leadership between ideal type and ideology. *Journal of Political Ideologies, 13*(1), 37–54.

Raynor, H. (Write), & Mackinnon, D. (Director). (2008, April 26). The Sontaran Stratagem (Season 4, Episode 4) [TV series episode]. In R. T. Davies & J. Gardner (Executive Producers), *Doctor Who*. BBC.

Raynor, H. (Writer), & Mackinnon, D. (Director). (2008, May 3). The Poison Sky (Season 4, Episode 5) [TV series episode]. In R. T. Davies & J. Gardner (Executive Producers), *Doctor Who*. BBC.

Raynor, H. (Writer), & Strong, J. (Director). (2007, April 21). Daleks in Manhattan (Season 3, Episode 4) [TV series episode]. In R. T. Davies & J. Gardner (Executive Producers), *Doctor Who*. BBC.

Roberts, A. (2007). *The history of science fiction*. Palgrave Macmillan.

Roberts, G. (Writer), & Palmer, C. (Director). (2007, April 7). The Shakespeare Code (Season 3, Episode 2) [TV series episode]. In R. T. Davies & J. Gardner (Executive Producers), *Doctor Who*. BBC.

Solomon, S., Greenberg, J., & Pyszczynski, T. (1998). Tales from the crypt: On the role of death in life. *Zygon, 33*(1), 9–43.

Sontag, S. (1976). The imagination of disaster. In M. Rose (Ed.), *Science fiction: A collection of critical essays*. Prentice-Hall.

Temple, K. (Writer), & Harper, G. (Director). (2008, April 19). Planet of the Ood (Season 4, Episode 2) [TV series episode]. In R. T. Davies & J. Gardner (Executive Producers), *Doctor Who*. BBC.

Tregenna, C. (Writer), & Bazalgette, E. (Director). (2015, October 24). The Woman Who Lived (Season 9, Episode 6) [TV series episode]. In S. Moffat & B. Minchin (Executive Producers), *Doctor Who*. BBC.

Uhl-Bien, M., Riggio, R. E., Lowe, K. B., & Carsten, M. K. (2014). Followership theory: A review and research agenda. *The Leadership Quarterly, 25*, 83–104.

Vondey, M. (2008). Follower-focused leadership: Effect of follower self-concepts and self-determination on organizational citizen behavior. *Emerging Leadership Journeys, 1*(1), 52–61.

Whitehouse, T. (Writer), & Campbell, J. (Director). (2010, May 8). The Vampires of Venice (Season 5, Episode 6) [TV series episode]. In S. Moffat, P. Wenger, & B. Willis (Executive Producers), *Doctor Who*. BBC.

Whithouse, T. (Writer), & O'Hara, D. (Director). (2015, October 3). Under the Lake (Season 9, Episode 3) [TV series episode]. In S. Moffat & B. Minchin (Executive Producers), *Doctor Who*. BBC.

Yilmaz, D., & Kiliçoğlu, G. (2013). Resistance to change and ways of reducing resistance in educational organizations. *European Journal of Research on Education, 1*(1), 14–21.

Yost, K. (2014). *From starship captains to galactic rebels: Leaders in science fiction television*. Rowman & Littlefield.

Yukl, G. (2006). *Leadership in organizations* (6th ed.). Pearson-Prentice Hall.

Zaleznik, A. (1965). The dynamics of subordinacy. *Harvard Business Review, 43*(3), 119–131.

INDEX

Printed in the USA
CPSIA information can be obtained
at www.ICGtesting.com
JSHW010841211223
54085JS00001B/1